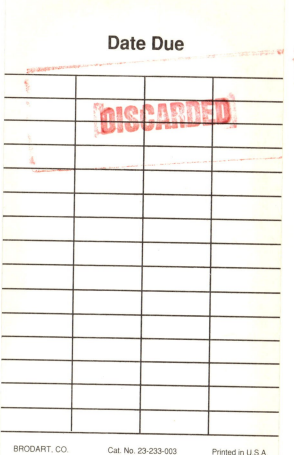

Date Due

BRODART, CO.   Cat. No. 23-233-003   Printed in U.S.A.

Justice Antonin Scalia and the Supreme Court's Conservative Moment

Justice Antonin Scalia
and the
Supreme Court's
Conservative Moment

CHRISTOPHER E. SMITH

Westport, Connecticut
London

Library of Congress Cataloging-in-Publication Data

Smith, Christopher E.
    Justice Antonin Scalia and the Supreme Court's conservative mo-
ment
/ Christopher E. Smith.
       p.   cm.
    Includes bibliographical references and index.
    ISBN 0–275–94705–X (alk. paper)
    1. Scalia, Antonin. 2. United States. Supreme Court.
3. Political questions and judicial power—United States.
4. Conservatism—United States.   I. Title.
KF8745.S33S65 1993
347.73'26—dc20   93–25057
[347.30735]

British Library Cataloguing in Publication Data is available.

Library of Congress Catalog Card Number: 93–25057
ISBN: 0–275–94705–X

First published in 1993

Praeger Publishers, 88 Post Road West, Westport, CT 06881
An imprint of Greenwood Publishing Group, Inc.

Printed in the United States of America

∞™

The paper used in this book complies with the
Permanent Paper Standard issued by the National
Information Standards Organization (Z39.48–1984).

10 9 8 7 6 5 4 3 2 1

For Peggy and Ernie Zimmer

Contents

Preface

Scholars who study the United States Supreme Court face special challenges in seeking to gain the information necessary for a comprehensive understanding of the high court's decision making. The justices who serve on the Supreme Court issue written opinions that formally present the Court's decisions and reasoning. However, these written opinions do not provide a complete picture of judicial decision-making processes. In order to protect the image and legitimacy of the judicial branch, the justices remain cloistered behind their marble columns and velvet curtains as they seek to perpetuate the myth that they merely interpret law rather than create public policy. Scholars are well aware that the justices do much more than interpret law. The papers and autobiographies of deceased justices, comments to the press by anonymous law clerks, and occasional anecdotes revealed by the justices themselves all provide clues about the interactions, strategic and otherwise, that shape Supreme Court decisions as the justices seek to persuade each other about desirable outcomes. The black robes of judicial office cannot eliminate the human attributes and motivations of the people appointed to sit on the nation's most authoritative court. However, because these human beings strive to remain

aloof and inaccessible, scholars must struggle to piece together and interpret the bits of available information that
shed light on the human processes of Supreme Court decision making.

This book represents an effort to assemble in a scholarly
fashion the available information about the human decision
makers on the Rehnquist-era Supreme Court. Because any
person with powers of persuasion can be highly influential
within a small deliberative body of nine people, it is important to seek understanding about how the interactions of the
individuals on the Supreme Court shape law and public
policy for the entire nation. Although the dearth of specific
information about the internal processes and interactions at
the Supreme Court makes it difficult for scholars to pro-
nounce definitive conclusions about the high court's decision-making processes, scholars have traditionally used
published opinions as well as anecdotal information to develop analytical inferences about the justices' behavior. Inevitably, such analyses invite criticism for failing to fit the
traditional systematic criteria of social science research.
When dealing with subjects who are relatively inaccessible
and purposefully obscured behind a symbolic facade, the
advancement of knowledge requires investigators to seize
every tool available in order to present analytical arguments
and evidence to the scholarly community. Thus, although
this book begins with an admission about the speculative
aspects of its arguments and evidence, readers should recognize the necessity of interpreting all available evidence,
firmly substantiated or otherwise, in the interest of advancing the collective understanding of the Rehnquist Court's
role in the American political system and the influence of
individual justices within the Supreme Court.

I am very grateful to three law journals for their generous
permission to incorporate within this book portions of several of my previously published articles concerning the Supreme Court. Material from the following articles is incorporated
by permission: "Justice Antonin Scalia and the Institutions of

American Government," *Wake Forest Law Review* 25 (1990): 783–809; "Justice Antonin Scalia and Criminal Justice Cases," *Kentucky Law Journal* 81 (1992–93): 187–212; "The Supreme Court in Transition: Assessing the Legitimacy of the Leading Legal Institution," *Kentucky Law Journal* 79 (1990–91): 317–346; and "Vigilance or Accommodation: The Changing Supreme Court and Religious Freedom," *Syracuse Law Review* 42 (1991): 893–944.

I am also grateful to several individuals for their assistance in developing my interpretive ideas concerning the Supreme Court. Thomas Hensley of Kent State University has spent many hours discussing the Rehnquist Court with me. Linda Fry assisted my research on freedom of religion. Scott Patrick Johnson worked with me on several projects concerning the behavior of individual justices.

This book is affectionately dedicated to my aunt and uncle, Peggy and Ernie Zimmer, who have supported me with a home-away-from-home during my travels and an extended family-away-from-home after I settled in Ohio.

1

The Supreme Court's Conservative Moment

The United States Supreme Court sits atop the hierarchy of the American legal system as the most authoritative institution in the federal government's judicial branch. Unlike Congress and the office of the president, which are composed of a myriad of agencies and committees and multiple layers of decision makers, the Supreme Court consists of only nine individual human beings. Because of its small size and the close interaction of the justices within its decision-making process, the Supreme Court is structured to provide opportunities for individual justices to influence the development of constitutional law and public policy significantly. Sometimes individual justices are influential because they cast decisive votes that determine case outcomes when the Court is closely divided over controversial issues. In 1991, for example, Justice David Souter had a significant influence over case outcomes during his first term on the high court because he cast the decisive fifth vote in eleven important cases in which the other justices were evenly split, four to four.[1] Alternatively, individual justices can be especially influential because of the force of their intellect and personality or because they are especially persuasive in communicating with their colleagues in the Court's decision-making process.

For example, prior to his retirement in 1990, Justice William Brennan was regarded by many observers as the "center of gravity" on the Court because of his "intellectual force [and] magnetic personality."[2]

When President Ronald Reagan appointed Antonin Scalia to the Supreme Court in 1986, Scalia possessed the intellectual qualities, clarity of thought, and outspokenness that seemed to make him a likely candidate to be an especially influential justice. According to one commentator, Scalia was "billed as the intellectual lodestar who would pull the Court to the right by the force of his brilliance."[3] As a former law professor noted for his intelligent, forceful opinions, Scalia showed that he intended to influence the shape of constitutional law and attendant public policies. Indeed, after seven terms on the high court, Scalia was described in the press as a "ferocious conservative with an acerbic pen" and "a force no liberal can match," so that President Bill Clinton's first Supreme Court appointment would have to be "a justice who can stand up to Scalia."[4] Unlike other justices who limit their contacts with the public to occasional formal speeches to lawyers and law students, it is "clear from [Scalia's] writing and tireless academic lecturing that he wants to leave his personal brand on the law."[5] In addition, Scalia served on the Court at a time when the political conservatives had gained the upper hand through the retirements of liberal Warren Court–era holdovers, especially Justices William Brennan and Thurgood Marshall, who were replaced by conservative appointees of Presidents Ronald Reagan and George Bush. Reagan and Bush selected their appointees with the hope that the new justices would replace liberal judicial policies with politically conservative decisions.

Scholars who study governmental actions on public policy issues describe "windows of opportunity" when particular issues rise on the policy agendas of governmental institutions and receive attention from authoritative decision makers. As described by John Kingdon, a "policy window" is an "opportunit[y] for action on given initiatives [that] presents [itself] and stays open for only short periods."[6] In an analogous context on the Supreme Court, the shifting composition of the high court created a window of opportunity for the newer conservative appointees of Presidents Reagan and Bush to undo the liberal doctrines and policies from the Warren and Burger Court eras. From 1987, when Reagan's appointment of Justice Anthony Kennedy tipped the balance on the Court in favor of political conservatives, to 1993, when the Democrats regained control of the White House and the judicial appointment process, the Supreme Court was in a conservative historical "moment" in which the justices could have drastically changed constitutional law and judicial policy making. Important Supreme Court decisions changed existing law concerning several policy issues, including abortion and criminal defendants' rights. However, the Court stopped short of a complete alteration of the high court's doctrines and role within the political system.

Justice Scalia was well suited and well positioned for the task of achieving his conservative goals, yet he had less influence on the Court than his admirers originally predicted and his critics continually feared. In the Supreme Court's modern moment of opportunity for conservative action, why did Scalia fail to lead or persuade his fellow conservatives in the Court's majority to undo the constitutional doctrines and judicial policies that he and other political conservatives had long criticized? The chapters that follow will address this question. Although this book will focus on the role of one individual within the Supreme Court, namely Justice Scalia, the analysis has implications for understanding decision making in the high court and the tendency of some justices to move toward moderation rather than to seek complete attainment of ideological goals.

SOCIAL CHANGE AND THE POLITICAL MOMENT

A single individual can have an important impact on history. In some instances, a charismatic or inspirational leader can single-handedly serve as a catalyst or architect of social change. Dr. Martin Luther King, Jr., for example, guided African-Americans' civil rights movement of the 1950s and 1960s through his abilities as an inspirational leader who combined firm moral commitment with a strategic sensitivity to the reactions of governmental leaders and white Americans generally.[7]

In the context of the United States Supreme Court, Earl Warren used his leadership abilities and persuasive skills to lead the high court on an unprecedented path of involvement in public policy issues during his service as chief justice from 1953 to 1969. Under Warren, the Supreme Court's image and role in the American political system changed as the Court became the governing system's institutional leader in both issuing symbolic declarations and shaping public policy for such issues as racial discrimination, criminal defendants' rights, and freedom of religion. For example, prior to Warren's arrival at the Supreme Court, the justices had been divided on how to address the issue of racial segregation in schools. Their uncertainty and reluctance about the issue was evident in their decision under Chief Justice Fred Vinson to delay any resolution while having the case scheduled for reargument the year after the Court had first heard oral arguments. After Vinson's death and the appointment of Warren, the governor of California, as chief justice, Warren persuaded the justices to issue a unanimous opinion condemning governmental policies of racial discrimination and declaring the practice unconstitutional. By persuading the justices to issue a unanimous opinion, Warren ensured that the Court maximized the weight of its institutional legitimacy and the effectiveness of its voice in the face of what was certain to be vocal opposition and confrontational resistance by political leaders in many parts of the country.[8]

In any leadership situation, whether in national governments, social movements, or specific institutional contexts, an individual's ability to have significant influence is limited by the existing social and political environment. Dr. King, for example, would have been much less effective in the 1920s. At that time, governmental leaders and American public opinion accepted and endorsed oppressive, discriminatory policies and had little concern about the pervasive victimization of African-Americans. In the 1950s, by contrast, racial attitudes were softening in segments of white society. Some American leaders recognized the hypocrisy of preaching freedom and equality to leaders of emerging Third World nations while practicing racial discrimination at home. Moreover, the changing industrial economy had new needs for African-American workers and thereby created opportunities for mobility for workers who had previously been trapped in traditional social and economic roles as agricultural laborers in southern states. In addition, a few national political leaders and institutions began their initial efforts to change patterns of racial discrimination. Presidents Franklin Delano Roosevelt and Harry S. Truman, for example, initiated and supervised the implementation of antidiscrimination laws for government contractors and the desegregation of the armed forces. Leaders of the national Democratic Party espoused civil rights principles. The Supreme Court accelerated its decisions against racial segregation. Thus, unlike in earlier decades, the social and political environment of the United States had changed to create the possibility of progress. In order words, a historical moment had arrived in which a leader with Dr. King's qualities and skills could have an important impact.

Similarly, on the Supreme Court, Chief Justice Warren's influence was possible only because the political composition of the Court's justices tilted in favor of Warren's values and policy preferences. Democratic appointees of President Roosevelt, especially Hugo Black and William O. Douglas, shared Warren's views about many civil rights and liberties issues. Republican President Dwight Eisenhower did not appoint politically conservative justices and, in fact, inadvertently appointed one of the most politically liberal justices ever to serve on the high court: Warren's close associate,

William Brennan. Liberal appointees by Presidents John F. Kennedy and Lyndon Johnson, including Arthur Goldberg, Abe Fortas, and Thurgood Marshall, gave Warren further support and cooperation in the 1960s. In addition, the Supreme Court's path-breaking decisions on civil rights and liberties during Warren's tenure were issued in an era in which the country was becoming increasingly receptive to the idea that individuals possess a variety of strong protections against governmental actions.

Warren's imprint on constitutional law and public policy contrasted sharply with the relative ineffectiveness of justices who espoused civil liberties before the appropriate historical moment had arrived. Justice John Harlan, for example, who was the grandfather of a namesake justice on the Warren Court, was a lonely advocate for the broad application of the Bill of Rights and the dismantling of racial segregation during the 1880s and 1890s. In the 1884 case of *Hurtado v. California*,[9] Harlan dissented from the majority's decision that the provisions of the Bill of Rights protect individuals only against infringements by the federal government and not those perpetrated by state and local governments. In his famous 1896 dissent in *Plessy v. Ferguson*,[10] Harlan declared that the "Constitution is color blind" and argued that racial segregation violated the principle of equal protection in the Constitution. Unfortunately for Harlan and American society, he was out of step with his times. Had he lived long enough, he would have seen many of his ideas about constitutional law come to fruition during the Warren era. The Supreme Court's 1954 decision in *Brown v. Board of Education*[11] invalidated state-sponsored racial segregation fifty-eight years after Harlan argued for that result. By the 1960s, the Supreme Court had applied most of the provisions of the Bill of Rights against state and local governments as well as against the federal government as Harlan had urged in *Hurtado*. Although constitutional law eventually reflected Harlan's ideas, because of the social and political environment of the United States at the end of the nineteenth century,

Harlan's liberal opinions on civil rights and liberties were merely seeds unsuccessfully planted in hostile soil.

DEVELOPMENTS PRECEDING SCALIA'S CONSERVATIVE MOMENT

The conservative justices' window of opportunity developed in reaction to the liberal decisions initiated by the Warren-era Supreme Court during the 1950s and 1960s. Under the leadership of Chief Justice Warren, the Supreme Court expanded the definitions of individuals' constitutional rights, expanded the application of those rights against state and local governments as well as the federal government, and undertook intrusive supervision of the policies and programs of government officials throughout the United States. The conservative backlash against the liberal judicial activism of the Warren Court produced judicial appointments in the 1970s, 1980s, and 1990s that were specifically intended by Presidents Richard Nixon, Reagan, and Bush to undo Supreme Court decisions affecting a variety of public policy issues.

When President Eisenhower appointed Warren to be chief justice in 1953, people throughout the country expected Warren's judicial behavior to reflect his solid Republican credentials and his experience as a tough prosecuting attorney in California. Warren was not known as an outspoken advocate of the rights of individuals. In fact, he was one of the primary architects of the shameful governmental policy during World War II of incarcerating innocent Japanese-American men, women, and children in concentration camps without any proof that they intended to assist, or even sympathized with, the Japanese government. Warren surprised Eisenhower and many other people by leading the Supreme Court to act assertively in expanding individuals' protections under the Bill of Rights. Eisenhower later referred to his appointments of Warren and Justice Brennan to the Supreme Court as the two biggest mistakes of his presidency.[12]

During the Warren era, the Supreme Court issued a variety of controversial decisions that protected the rights of individuals and simultaneously limited the authority of government officials. Several famous cases illustrate Warren Court actions that generated controversy and criticism. In *Brown v. Board of Education* (1954),[13] the Court unleashed a fire storm of controversy by declaring that government-sponsored racial discrimination violated the Constitution's equal protection principles. Enforcement of the decision by lower court judges seeking to end racial segregation in public schools led to howls of protest by southern politicians and violent resistance in several cities.

The justices shocked the nation in 1962 by declaring that public schools could not sponsor prayers in classrooms (*Engel v. Vitale*).[14] The justices concluded that such prayers violated the First Amendment's Establishment Clause by manifesting improper government support for religion. Although many mainline churches supported the Court's decision, millions of Americans disagreed with what they perceived to be the Supreme Court's effort to remove the influence of God from children's lives. After the Court's decision, public schools in many regions of the country defied the new judicial policy.[15] In addition, legislators in many states continually challenged the decision by enacting laws intended to bring Christian religion into public school classrooms through silent prayers, posting the Ten Commandments, and other devices that eventually were invalidated in later judicial decisions.

Griswold v. Connecticut (1965) created a controversial right to privacy even though the word *privacy* is not mentioned anywhere in the Constitution.[16] In other controversial decisions, the Supreme Court also supported congressional efforts to prohibit racial discrimination by businesses,[17] endorsed civil rights protestors' right to stage marches,[18] and provided judicial protection for welfare recipients[19] and prisoners.[20]

Chief Justice Warren did not support liberal outcomes in all of the Court's decisions, but his leadership role facilitated the development of the Supreme Court into an institution actively involved in policy issues through the interpretation of individuals' constitutional rights.

A series of decisions during the 1960s aroused the ire of politicians and the public by expanding constitutional protections for criminal defendants. In *Mapp v. Ohio* (1961),[21] the Warren-era justices applied the "exclusionary rule" to forbid state and local law enforcement officials from using improperly obtained evidence against criminal suspects. In *Gideon v. Wainwright* (1963),[22] the Court decreed that indigent criminal defendants facing incarceration must be provided with defense attorneys to represent them at state expense. The Court also required police officers to inform suspects of their rights to remain silent and to be represented by counsel (*Miranda v. Arizona*, 1966).[23] Police chiefs throughout the country complained that the Supreme Court was preventing law enforcement officials from arresting, prosecuting, and punishing criminals by creating rules for police behavior that protected the interests of guilty individuals rather than the interests of society. Many members of the Warren Court had personal knowledge of abusive behavior by law enforcement officials early in the twentieth century, and they sought to prevent abuses by creating rules for police behavior.[24] However, because these rules were created during the 1960s when crime rates grew and the American public was increasingly concerned about social conflict, urban riots, and political protests over civil rights and the Vietnam War, many political conservatives believed that the Court had gone too far in defining individual rights and thereby intruding on the policies and practices of local officials.

As the Republican candidate for the presidency in 1968, Richard Nixon attempted to cultivate conservative voters and southern white voters by criticizing controversial judicial policies—such as busing for school desegregation and criminal defendants' rights—that were unpopular with those segments of the electorate. When he became president, Nixon attempted to use his appointments to the Supreme Court to cater to these important constituencies. Because of strategic mistakes by President Johnson in attempting to elevate his close friend Justice Abe Fortas to replace retiring Chief Justice Warren, Nixon ultimately was able to fill four vacancies on the Supreme Court with his appointees.[25] Nixon made appointments to replace retiring Warren Court members Hugo Black and John Harlan as well as the appointment to replace Chief Justice Warren, whose retirement was planned during the Johnson presidency. In addition, Nixon selected the replacement for Justice Fortas, whose resignation stemmed from revelations about his personal finances generated by Johnson's nomination fiasco.

Nixon sought to appoint judicial conservatives whose opinions would undo the liberal decisions and judicial policies produced by the Warren Court justices. Nixon's appointee to be chief justice, Warren Burger, had distinguished himself as a tough "law and order" judge who was critical of Warren-era decisions expanding constitutional protections for criminal defendants. Nixon appointee William Rehnquist, who would later become chief justice during the Reagan administration, had helped to carry out the Nixon administration's crackdowns and surveillance on antiwar protestors while serving in the Justice Department. Lewis Powell, Nixon's southern appointee, had a reputation as a political moderate, but his voting record ultimately demonstrated that he regularly cast conservative votes in civil rights and liberties decisions.[26] Nixon's fourth appointee, Harry Blackmun, a federal judge from Minnesota and longtime friend of Warren Burger, initially voted consistently with the conservatives before gradually changing his views over the years to become a frequent ally of liberal justices.

During Chief Justice Burger's tenure, the Nixon appointees needed to attract only one vote from Warren-era holdovers in order to form decisive majorities. Frequently, they could gain that vote from either Justice Potter Stewart,

Republican appointee of President Eisenhower, or Justice Byron White, an appointee of President Kennedy who often opposed the Warren Court's liberal decisions on criminal justice. The Burger Court decided several important cases that blocked judicial policy initiatives favored by the liberals (i.e., Brennan, Marshall, and Douglas) remaining on the Supreme Court from the Warren era. For example, by a narrow five-to-four vote, the Nixon appointees plus Justice Stewart limited the scope of school desegregation remedies in 1974 by declaring that busing must generally be limited to the boundaries of single school districts, even if racial segregation in the district was fostered by state governmental action and the segregation could not be remedied within the single district alone.[27] The previous year the same five-member majority halted federal judicial initiatives to equalize funding for rich and poor students in public schools by declaring that the Constitution does not forbid wealth discrimination and that education is not a fundamental right for American children.[28] Later during the Burger era, after retiring Warren-era Justices Douglas and Stewart had been replaced by appointees of Presidents Ford and Reagan (i.e., John Paul Stevens and Sandra Day O'Connor, respectively), the justices reversed the Court's direction on issues affecting criminal defendants' rights. For example, the Burger-era majority created exceptions to the "exclusionary rule" and thereby effectively relaxed judicial supervision of police behavior during warrantless searches.[29]

Although the Burger Court majority was more conservative than the Warren-era Supreme Court's justices, the newer justices did not undertake a wholesale reversal of decisions and judicial policies generated by the high court under Chief Justice Warren. Many political conservatives were deeply disappointed because the post-Warren Republican appointees did not abolish busing for school desegregation, they maintained the judicial ban on organized prayer in public schools, and they preserved the *Miranda* rule and essential aspects of the controversial "exclusionary rule."

Conservatives were doubly disappointed because the Burger-era Supreme Court enunciated new constitutional rights and made liberal decisions affecting other issues. Most notably, three Nixon appointees joined four Warren-era hold-overs in 1973 to produce the most controversial opinion of Supreme Court history in *Roe v. Wade*, the decision recognizing a woman's constitutional right of choice for abortion. The decision spawned a significant backlash from political conservatives and mobilized interest groups opposed to abortion. The Court also endorsed the controversial policy of affirmative action in university admissions and job hiring. In addition, the Burger Court expanded the scope of rights for convicted criminal offenders and facilitated judicial supervision of state correctional institutions that were found to have conditions of confinement in violation of the Eighth Amendment's prohibition on cruel and unusual punishments.[30] Because the Burger Court did not actively reverse many of the controversial Warren-era precedents, some scholars have wondered "whether the Burger Court was only a transition from the liberal activism of the Warren Court to the reactionary activism of the Rehnquist Court."[31]

The opportunity for political conservatives to control the Supreme Court and potentially reverse the trends initiated by the Warren Court came with the election of Ronald Reagan to the presidency in 1980. Reagan captured the Republican Party nomination with the strong support of antiabortion groups, conservative religious leaders, and others who were critical of the Supreme Court's decisions on such issues as abortion, criminal defendants' rights, school prayer, and affirmative action. Reagan's election was facilitated by President Jimmy Carter's negative image in the eyes of many voters, the Iranian hostage crisis that made President Carter appear to be politically impotent, and a relatively strong showing by moderate independent candidate John Anderson, who siphoned votes away from Carter.[32] Reagan was not elected because a majority of Americans wanted him to fight against liberal public policies shaped by the Supreme

Court. Indeed, public opinion polls consistently showed that a majority of Americans disagreed with Reagan's steadfast opposition to a right of choice for abortion. However, because a majority of voters did not want to reelect President Carter and Reagan happened to be the alternative candidate offered by the Republican Party, the electorate placed in the White House a stridently conservative administration that was intent on changing the ideological composition of the federal judiciary, especially the Supreme Court.

During the Reagan administration's eight years in office and the subsequent four-year presidency of Reagan's vice president, George Bush, conservative Republicans never succeeded in their efforts to enact statutes and constitutional amendments that would reverse liberal Supreme Court decisions on abortion, school prayer, affirmative action, and other issues. Because Democrats always controlled one or both houses of Congress during the Reagan and Bush presidencies, political conservatives enjoyed only limited success in reshaping social policy through actions by the legislative branch.

Reagan's and Bush's most successful efforts to alter social policy came through their systematic efforts to appoint strongly conservative judicial officers to life-tenured positions as federal district and circuit judges and Supreme Court justices. According to Sheldon Goldman, the Reagan administration "engaged in the most systematic ideological or judicial philosophical screening of judicial candidates since the first Roosevelt administration."[33] Many moderate Republicans were excluded from consideration for judgeships despite their longtime loyalty to their political party. Bush's administration subsequently emulated Reagan's efforts to ensure that judicial appointees held appropriately conservative views about controversial social issues.[34] By 1993, Presidents Reagan and Bush had appointed two thirds of the nation's federal judges.

By emphasizing the appointment of young judges, including some in their early thirties who could potentially make authoritative decisions for nearly half a century, Presidents Reagan and Bush also sought to ensure that their judicial appointees would have influence over law and policy long after these conservative presidents had left the White House.[35] This strategy was also applied to appointees for the Supreme Court. Unlike President Nixon, who appointed Justice Powell when Powell was in his sixties, Presidents Reagan and Bush appointed justices whom they presumed would serve on the high court and shape judicial decisions for decades to come. Justices Sandra O'Connor, Antonin Scalia, Anthony Kennedy, and David Souter were each appointed to the Supreme Court not long after turning fifty, and Justice Clarence Thomas was only forty-three when he began his service on the Rehnquist Court.

THE CONSERVATIZATION OF THE SUPREME COURT

In their initial performances on the Supreme Court, each of the five justices appointed by Presidents Reagan and Bush demonstrated that they were more conservative on controversial social issues than the retiring justices they replaced.

Moderate Republican Justice Potter Stewart retired in 1981 and was replaced by Reagan appointee Justice Sandra Day O'Connor. Although Stewart had been a member of the original seven-member majority that established the right of choice for abortion in *Roe v. Wade*,[36] O'Connor issued a strong critique of the reasoning in *Roe*[37] and consistently supported state-imposed limitations on abortion that were vigorously opposed by the remaining members of the original *Roe* majority, Justices Blackmun, Brennan, and Marshall.[38] Stewart was the author of an important opinion endorsing congressional power under the Thirteenth Amendment to permit racial discrimination lawsuits to be filed against private citizens who engage in certain kinds of discrimination.[39] By contrast, O'Connor supported her conservative colleagues' efforts to limit the application of such laws and thereby make it more difficult for people to file discrimination cases in the federal courts.[40] In addition, O'Connor's support for the application of criminal sanctions to prohibit the burning of the American flag as a means of political expression[41] appeared to clash with Stewart's role in a case overturning the conviction of a man who burned a flag to protest civil rights issues during the 1960s.[42] Thus, O'Connor's appointment provided a new conservative voice within a Court dominated by holdover justices appointed by President Nixon and his predecessors.

As Chapter 2 will discuss in greater detail, Justice Scalia's appointment in 1986 upon the retirement of Chief Justice Burger provided the Court with an articulate, outspoken member who was more consistently conservative than his predecessor. For example, Chief Justice Burger authored important opinions endorsing Congress's statutory affirmative action program for the awarding of federal government contracts to minority business enterprises.[43] By contrast, Scalia established himself as an outspoken critic of affirmative action before being appointed to the Supreme Court,[44] and he dissented from a subsequent decision endorsing federal affirmative action efforts in awarding broadcast licenses.[45] Chief Justice Burger also authored the opinion explaining appropriate burdens of proof for employment discrimination lawsuits,[46] while Scalia joined four other justices in later sharply restricting Burger's initial decision.[47]

Justice Anthony Kennedy, whom Reagan appointed to fill the vacancy created by the retirement of Justice Lewis Powell in 1987, was notably more conservative than Powell on two of the burning issues of the day, abortion and affirmative action. On abortion, Powell was a member of the original *Roe* majority in 1973. In 1983, Powell issued an open plea to his colleagues to leave the abortion precedent intact in order to ensure the stability of law for society rather than change the controversial judicial policy simply because the composition of the Court had changed.[48] Kennedy, by contrast, joined the justices who were willing to permit state regulation of abortion and who criticized the reasoning in *Roe*.[49] On affirmative action, Powell crafted the careful compromise opinion in *Regents of the University of California v. Bakke* (1978)[50] that struck down racial quotas in medical school admissions but permitted race to be considered as one factor in admissions decisions because of the benefits of diversity for a medical school's student body. Kennedy actively opposed affirmative action by joining the majority opinion that struck down the city of Richmond's minority contract program[51] and by dissenting vigorously against the continuation of the Federal Communication Commission's affirmative action policies in awarding broadcast licenses.[52]

In 1990, one of the most consistently liberal holdovers from the Warren era, Justice William Brennan, retired from the Supreme Court. President Bush appointed Justice David Souter, a relatively unknown former member of the New Hampshire Supreme Court, to replace one of the leading liberals in the Court's history. During his confirmation hearings, Souter responded to questions in a generally vague manner and thereby effectively avoided senators' efforts to have him publicly define his judicial philosophy.[53] Souter's first-term performance, however, showed that he was much more conservative than his liberal predecessor. Souter cast the decisive fifth vote in eleven cases that would have been decided the other way if Justice Brennan had remained on the Court.[54] These cases included seven decisions concerning the rights of criminal defendants and prisoners, two cases concerning freedom of speech, and two cases concerning labor relations and civil litigation.[55]

Justice Clarence Thomas, Bush's appointee to the Court in 1991, proved to be much more conservative than his predecessor, Justice Thurgood Marshall, who was one of the most liberal holdovers from the Warren Court era. Although Thomas attempted to evade questions about his judicial philosophy posed by members of the Senate Judiciary Committee during his confirmation hearings,[56] his record as an official in the Reagan administration included many speeches and articles critical of liberal judicial decisions on such issues as affirmative action, abortion, and school prayer. During his first term on the Court, Thomas supported conservative outcomes so consistently that he formed a discernible voting bloc with the Supreme Court's two most conservative justices, Justice Scalia and Chief Justice Rehnquist. Thomas agreed with Scalia in 79 percent of nonunanimous cases and with Rehnquist in 74 percent of such cases.[57] By contrast, during the preceding term, Thomas's predecessor, Justice Marshall, agreed with Scalia in only 29 percent of nonunanimous cases and with Rehnquist in only 17 percent of such cases.[58]

The appointment of Justice Kennedy in 1988 gave the conservatives a five-member majority composed of Chief Justice Rehnquist, Justice Scalia, Justice O'Connor, Justice Kennedy, and Justice White for issues such as criminal defendants' rights and abortion in which each had regularly favored conservative outcomes. By 1991, the conservatives had the clear potential to change constitutional law and judicial policy making as they wished because the five-member majority had been strengthened by the addition of Bush appointees, Justices Souter and Thomas. The lone Democrat and Warren-era holdover on the Court was Justice White, a frequent ally of the conservatives. The Court's two most liberal justices, Justice Blackmun and Justice Stevens, had traditionally supported conservative outcomes frequently enough for issues such as, respectively, criminal defendants' rights and affirmative action to be considered as merely moderates in comparison with such Warren Court liberal stalwarts as Justices Brennan, Marshall, Douglas, and Goldberg.

The Supreme Court's conservative moment was achieved not only through the alteration of the Court's composition but also through the actions of interest groups, states, and the federal government in presenting cases to the high court. The Supreme Court cannot easily reach out to seize issues for consideration merely because the issues are of interest to some justices who wish to change the state of constitutional law. Cases must be brought to the Supreme Court after working their way through the lower courts. It is a very expensive and time-consuming process to initiate litigation and sustain it through all the stages of a state or federal court system. The Supreme Court's transformed composition gave conservative interest groups and state and local governments a strong incentive to pursue cases challenging liberal judicial principles established during the Warren and Burger eras.

Because they sensed the opportunity to seek changes in precedents with which they disagreed, attorneys for local governments and interest groups fed the Court a steady flow of case offerings from which to select issues to be decided in the highest court. State and local governments, for example, passed laws limiting the availability of abortion that flew in the face of established precedent in order to supply the new justices with appropriate vehicles to use in overturning *Roe v. Wade*. Similarly, in the context of criminal justice, police officers, prosecutors, and state trial judges tested Supreme Court precedents concerning searches, jury selection procedures, and jury instructions with the hope that the new conservative majority would relax protections for criminal defendants and increase the discretionary authority of criminal justice officials.

In addition, the Reagan and Bush administrations used the Office of the Solicitor General, the official responsible for representing the federal government in the Supreme Court, to urge the conservative justices to change established precedents concerning abortion, school desegregation, affirmative action, and criminal defendants' rights.[59] Social science research indicates that there is a strong correlation between recommendations to the Supreme Court by the solicitor general and the selection of cases for hearing and decision by the justices.[60] Thus, by turning the solicitor general into a conservative policy advocate, especially during the Reagan administration, the conservative presidential administrations controlling the executive branch of the federal government could assist and encourage the new Supreme Court majority in reexamining liberal judicial decisions affecting civil rights and liberties.

The new conservative majority flexed its muscles and rewrote constitutional law and statutory interpretation to advance conservative outcomes in many cases. For example, although their decisions on discrimination law were later reversed by congressional enactments, in 1989 the conservatives quickly revised interpretations of federal employment discrimination laws to make it more difficult for discrimination victims to win lawsuits and recover financial damages from employers.[61] By using reasoning and conclusions that the original *Roe* majority would never have accepted, the conservative justices also invited states to regulate and limit women's opportunities to obtain abortions.[62] In 1991, the new majority also overruled precedents that were only two and four years old in order to give juries greater discretion to apply the death penalty by relying on subjective assessments of emotional and other distress suffered by crime victims' families.[63]

Despite these cases and other examples of decisions that constricted the scope of individual rights, by the time Democrats regained control of the White House and authority over federal judicial appointments in 1993, the essential core of many liberal judicial principles established by the Warren and Burger Courts remained intact. Abortion remained legal and available throughout the country. Police were still required to read suspects their *Miranda* warnings. The "exclusionary rule" continued to exist, albeit in a narrower form, to deter police from many kinds of overzealous, warrantless searches. Public schools were still barred from organizing prayers in their classrooms. The Burger Court never initiated a conservative counterrevolution because of the moderation of many of its Republican appointees and because the Supreme Court still contained several liberal holdovers from the Warren Court era. Under Chief Justice Rehnquist, however, the Court's composition had changed to give judicial conservatives numerical dominance, yet the counterrevolution desired by Presidents Reagan and Bush and their supporters did not occur when the moment of opportunity presented itself.

The central argument of this book is that Justice Scalia, the creative, brilliant, and outspoken intellectual leader of the Court's conservative majority, made a pivotal contribution to the failure of the judicial counterrevolution that he so fervently sought to achieve. As subsequent chapters will explain, Scalia's philosophy, behavior, and style made him an ineffective coalition builder within the political decision-making processes of a collegial court in which it takes five votes to establish a new precedent. Within the dynamic mixture of the Rehnquist Court justices' personalities and decision-making processes, Scalia shared with his conservative colleagues similar assessments about case outcomes. However, his strident efforts to push for those outcomes also served to push some of his erstwhile allies toward a moderate stance on key issues that was neither entirely predictable from their judicial philosophies nor consistent with their conservative decisions in other cases.

NOTES

1. Scott P. Johnson and Christopher E. Smith, "David Souter's First Term on the Supreme Court: The Impact of a New Justice," *Judicature* 75 (1992): 239.

2. Linda Greenhouse, "An Activist's Legacy," *New York Times*, 22 July 1990, pp. 1, 22.

3. Tony Mauro, "High Court Adjourns for the Summer Intact," *Legal Times*, 9 July 1990, p. 10.

4. "An Antidote to Antonin," *Newsweek*, 29 March 1993, p. 23.

5. David Kaplan and Bob Cohn, "The Court's Mr. Right," *Newsweek*, 5 November 1990, p. 67.

6. John W. Kingdon, *Agendas, Alternatives, and Public Policies* (Boston: Little, Brown, 1984), p. 174.

7. See Taylor Branch, *Parting the Waters: America in the King Years 1954–1963* (New York: Simon and Schuster, 1988).

8. Richard Kluger, *Simple Justice: The History of Brown v. Board of Education and Black America's Struggle for Equality* (New York: Random House, 1975), pp. 694–709.

9. Hurtado v. California, 110 U.S. 516 (1884).

10. Plessy v. Ferguson, 163 U.S. 537 (1896).

11. Brown v. Board of Education, 347 U.S. 483 (1954).

12. Henry J. Abraham, *Justices and Presidents: A Political History of Appointments to the Supreme Court,* 2nd ed. (New York: Oxford University Press, 1985), p. 263.

13. Brown v. Board of Education, 347 U.S. 483 (1954).

14. Engel v. Vitale, 370 U.S. 421 (1962).

15. Kenneth M. Dolbeare and Phillip E. Hammond, "Inertia at Midway: Supreme Court Decisions and Local Responses," *Journal of Legal Education* 23 (1970): 112–116.

16. Griswold v. Connecticut, 381 U.S. 479 (1965).

17. Katzenbach v. McClung, 379 U.S. 294 (1964).

18. Edwards v. South Carolina, 372 U.S. 229 (1963).

19. Shapiro v. Thompson, 394 U.S. 618 (1969).

20. Cooper v. Pate, 378 U.S. 546 (1964).

21. Mapp v. Ohio, 367 U.S. 643 (1961).

22. Gideon v. Wainwright, 372 U.S. 335 (1963).

23. Miranda v. Arizona, 384 U.S. 436 (1966).

24. Christopher E. Smith, "Police Professionalism and the Rights of Criminal Defendants," *Criminal Law Bulletin* 26 (1990): 155–166.

25. Christopher E. Smith, " 'What If. . . .': Critical Junctures on the Road to (In)Equality," *Thurgood Marshall Law Review* 15 (1989–90): 10–17.

26. Janet Blasecki, "Justice Lewis F. Powell: Swing Voter or Staunch Conservative?" *Journal of Politics* 52 (1990): 530–547.

27. Milliken v. Bradley, 418 U.S. 717 (1974).

28. San Antonio Independent School District v. Rodriguez, 411 U.S. 1 (1973).

29. United States v. Leon, 468 U.S. 897 (1984) ("good faith" exception); New York v. Quarles, 467 U.S. 649 (1984) (public safety exception).

30. Christopher E. Smith, "Federal Judges' Role in Prisoner Litigation: What's Necessary? What's Proper?" *Judicature* 70 (1986): 144–150.

31. Herman Schwartz, "Introduction," in *The Burger Years*, ed. Herman Schwartz (New York: Penguin, 1988), p. xxv.

32. Richard Kolbe, *American Political Parties: An Uncertain Future* (New York: Harper & Row, 1985), p. 209.

33. Sheldon Goldman, "Reagan's Second Term Judicial Appointments: The Battle at Midway," *Judicature* 70 (1987): 326.

34. Neil A. Lewis, "Bush Travels Reagan's Course in Naming Judges," *New York Times*, 10 April 1990, p. A1; Ruth Marcus, "Using the Bench to Bolster a Conservative Team," *Washington Post National Weekly Edition*, 25 February–3 March 1991, p. 31.

35. Herman Schwartz, *Packing the Courts: The Conservative Campaign to Rewrite the Constitution* (New York: Charles Scribners' Sons, 1988), pp. 90–95.

36. Roe v. Wade, 410 U.S. 113 (1973).

37. City of Akron v. Akron Center for Reproductive Health, 462 U.S. 416, 453 (1983) (O'Connor, J., dissenting).

38. Webster v. Reproductive Health Services, 109 S. Ct. 3040, 3058 (O'Connor, J., concurring).

39. Jones v. Alfred H. Mayer Co., 392 U.S. 409 (1968).

40. Patterson v. McLean Credit Union, 491 U.S. 164 (1989).

41. Texas v. Johnson, 109 S. Ct. 2533 (1989); United States v. Eichman, 110 S. Ct. 2404 (1990).

42. Street v. New York, 394 U.S. 576 (1969).

43. Fullilove v. Klutznick, 448 U.S. 448 (1980).

44. Antonin Scalia, "The Disease as Cure," *Washington University Law Quarterly* (1979): 147.

45. Metro Broadcasting Co. v. F.C.C., 110 S. Ct. 2997 (1990).

46. Griggs v. Duke Power Co., 401 U.S. 424 (1971).

47. Wards Cove Packing Co. v. Atonio, 490 U.S. 642 (1989).

48. City of Akron v. Akron Center for Reproductive Health, 462 U.S. 416, 421 n. 1 (1983).

49. Webster v. Reproductive Health Services, 109 S. Ct. 3040 (1989).

50. Regents of the University of California v. Bakke, 438 U.S. 265 (1978).

51. City of Richmond v. J. A. Croson Co., 488 U.S. 469 (1989).

52. Metro Broadcasting v. F.C.C., 110 S. Ct. 2997 (1990).

53. Linda Greenhouse, "Souter Tacks Over Shoals," *New York Times*, 14 September 1990, p. B5.

54. Christopher E. Smith and Scott P. Johnson, "Newcomer on the High Court: Justice Souter and the Supreme Court's 1990 Term," *South Dakota Law Review* 37 (1992): 39–41.

55. Arizona v. Fulminante, 111 S. Ct. 1246 (1991) (coerced confession may be regarded as "harmless error"); County of Riverside v. McLaughlin, 111 S. Ct. 1661 (1991) (arrestees may be held for forty-eight hours without being charged with a crime); Wilson v. Seiter, 111 S. Ct. 2321 (1991) (subjective rather than objective standard for determining unconstitutional conditions of confinement in correctional institutions); Harmelin v. Michigan, 111 S. Ct. 2680 (1991) (not cruel and unusual punishment to impose mandatory sentence of life without possibility of parole on first offender convicted of possessing large amount of cocaine); Mu'min v. Virginia, 111 S. Ct. 1899 (1991) (right to fair trial not violated when judge refused to question jurors about contents of newspaper report to which they had been exposed); Schad v. Arizona, 111 S. Ct. 2491 (1991) (approve judge's failure to instruct jury on lesser included offenses in capital case); Peretz v. United States, 111 S. Ct. 2661 (1991) (U.S. magistrate judges may conduct voir dire in felony cases without specific statutory authority); Barnes v. Glen Theatre Inc., 111 S. Ct. 2456 (1991) (state may ban nude dancing in bars even though such activity is recognized as nonobscene artistic expression); Rust v. Sullivan, 111 S. Ct. 1759 (1991) (federal government can forbid doctors in federally funded family planning clinics to discuss abortion with patients); Litton Financial Printing Div. v. National Labor Relations Board, 111 S. Ct. 2215 (1991) (layoff dispute is not governed by contractual grievance procedures after a labor contract has expired); Business Guides, Inc. v. Chromatic Communications Enterprises, Inc., 111 S. Ct. 922 (1991) (objective standard of reasonable inquiry applies to represented party for determination of Rule 11 sanctions under the Federal Rules of Civil Procedure).

56. Ruth Marcus, "Haven't We Met Before?: If You Liked the Souter Hearings, Then You Loved the Thomas Replay," *Washington Post National Weekly Edition*, 23 September–29 September 1991, p. 14.

57. Christopher E. Smith and Scott Patrick Johnson, "The First-Term Performance of Justice Clarence Thomas," *Judicature* 76 (1993): 174.

58. Johnson and Smith, "David Souter's First Term," p. 239.

59. Lincoln Caplan, *The Tenth Justice: The Solicitor General and the Rule of Law* (New York: Random House, 1987), pp. 51–64, 235–254.

60. Joseph Tanenhaus, Marvin Schick, Matthew Muraskin, and Daniel Rosen, "The Supreme Court's *Certiorari* Jurisdiction: Cue Theory," in *American Court Systems*, 2nd ed., eds. Sheldon Goldman and Austin Sarat (New York: Longman, 1989), pp. 158–165.

61. Christopher E. Smith, "The Supreme Court and Ethnicity," *Oregon Law Review* 69 (1990): 823–839.

62. Webster v. Reproductive Health Services, 109 S. Ct. 3040 (1989).

63. Payne v. Tennessee, 111 S. Ct. 2597 (1991).

2

Justice Antonin Scalia

Justice Antonin Scalia became an influential member of the Supreme Court because of his creative and outspoken opinions. However, as subsequent chapters of this book will discuss in greater detail, his judicial behavior also served to prevent the attainment of political conservatives' goals for the Supreme Court during their modern moment of opportunity for reversing the decisional trends established during the liberal Warren Court era. The purpose of this chapter is to introduce Justice Scalia by providing a general overview of the central themes that compose his judicial philosophy and that motivate his decision making as a justice on the Supreme Court. This presentation is intended merely as a general description of Scalia's philosophy and decisions. Because the central focus of the book is on the reactions to, and consequences of, Scalia's judicial behavior within the Supreme Court, this chapter does not purport to provide an exhaustive analysis of Scalia's judicial philosophy. Instead, it provides a basis for understanding Scalia's role and influence in the judicial politics of Supreme Court decision making.

SCALIA'S BACKGROUND

Antonin Scalia was born in 1936 and grew up in New York where his father was a professor of Romance languages at Brooklyn College. He was educated at Georgetown University and Harvard Law School. He practiced law with a large law firm in Cleveland, Ohio, for eight years before becoming a law professor at the University of Virginia's law school. During the Nixon administration, he was an attorney in the Justice Department, and during the Ford administration, he served as an assistant attorney general in the Office of Legal Counsel.[1] When the Democrats regained control of the White House in 1977, Scalia became a law professor at the University of Chicago and also served as editor of the conservative American Enterprise Institute's journal entitled *Regulation*.[2]

During his academic and government careers, he became known as an advocate of deregulation and increased power for the executive branch, two ideas reflecting his criticism of the exercises of authority by the Democrat-controlled Congress. He was also critical of liberal Supreme Court decisions, most notably the *Bakke* decision that endorsed the use of affirmative action—a decision that Professor Antonin Scalia in 1979 labeled as "an embarrassment to teach."[3]

In 1982, President Reagan appointed Scalia to be a judge on the U.S. Circuit Court of Appeals for the District of Columbia Circuit, the most prestigious federal appellate court that has special responsibilities for litigation challenging actions by federal executive branch agencies. When Chief Justice Warren Burger retired in 1986 and Reagan elevated the Court's most conservative jurist, Justice William Rehnquist, to be the new chief justice, Scalia was nominated to fill the vacancy as a new associate justice. President Reagan appointed Scalia to the Supreme Court not only because he was impressed with Scalia's record as a bright, energetic, and consistent conservative but also because he sought to claim credit with ethnic voters for appointing the first Italian-American to the high court.

During his confirmation hearings before the Senate Judiciary Committee, Scalia was spared the intense scrutiny and political conflict that derailed the nomination of his conservative colleague Judge Robert Bork the following year. Although representatives of liberal interest groups testified against Scalia's nomination, he was able to win an overwhelming confirmation vote in the Senate while generally avoiding providing detailed, specific answers to questions posed by members of the Judiciary Committee.

There are two primary reasons for Scalia's relatively easy confirmation proceedings. First, he was regarded as a conservative replacing another conservative, namely Chief Justice Burger. Thus, Scalia's nomination was not perceived as changing the ideological balance of power on the high court. Bork, by contrast, was nominated to replace Justice Lewis Powell, a supporter of abortion rights and the architect of compromise opinions approving affirmative action in some contexts. Therefore, liberal senators feared that Bork would tilt the Court too far in favor of conservative decisions. Although Scalia's appointment did not change the numerical distribution of liberals and conservatives on the Supreme Court, it was not true that Scalia was simply one conservative replacing another. Unlike his immediate predecessor, Chief Justice Burger, who was sometimes criticized for his inability to provide intellectual influence over the Court's opinions,[4] Scalia quickly became renowned for his innovative thinking and influential opinions. Scalia was often influential even when his views did not immediately prevail with a majority on the Court: "[Scalia's] willingness to discard accepted rules and refashion them in light of his own constitutional vision made his impact greater than his rather low success rate [as the author of majority opinions] might suggest."[5]

Second, liberal interest groups devoted their greatest attention to fighting against the nomination of William Rehnquist for chief justice. Because Scalia's nomination and confirmation hearings occurred at the same time as Rehnquist's appointment to be chief justice, liberal interests that might normally have scrutinized Scalia more closely and contested his nomination more vigorously were distracted in a fight against the justice (i.e., Rehnquist) who was clearly established as the Court's more conservative decision maker.

SCALIA'S CENTRAL THEMES

Justice Scalia is not a simple judicial conservative in the sense of someone who merely finds ways to rationalize support for politically conservative judicial outcomes. Instead, Scalia "possesses a judicial philosophy and political vision that extends far beyond simple allegiance to a few policy positions. . . . [I]t is a vision that limits the checking function of the Court in constitutional politics, enhances legislative and executive and agency power, and subjects rights to definition by the majority in control of government."[6] Scalia has actively sought to eliminate what he views as the Supreme Court's involvement in politics. For Scalia, attainment of this overriding goal involves reducing judicial involvement in public policy issues so that such issues can be left to the decisions of elected officials in the legislative and executive branches of government. It also involves adopting decision-making techniques that limit judicial officers' opportunities to impose their own values in determining case outcomes.

Scalia is subject to criticism for failing to follow his own guiding principles with respect to some issues. For example, he participated in conservative justices' efforts to rewrite both established employment discrimination laws[7] and rules for reviewing convicted offenders' habeas corpus petitions in the federal courts,[8] two statutory matters over which elected representatives in Congress rather than the appointed justices on the Supreme Court possess the ultimate authority. In general, however, these principles are underlying elements in the central themes that shape Scalia's decision making.

Constitutional Interpretation

Supreme Court justices frequently do not espouse or manifest in their decision making any particular theory of constitutional interpretation. In making decisions about cases heard by the Court, they obviously have to make choices about how they will interpret specific provisions of the Constitution. They may, however, make essentially ad hoc decisions about specific provisions of the nation's fundamental document without seeking to have their opinions guided by an overriding vision of the document's meaning. Frequently, their decisions may be guided by what many regard as "policy" decisions in that they balance competing interests while making value judgments and predictions about the consequences for society of particular judicial outcomes.[9] For example, in a 1971 case challenging state governments' policies of providing financial assistance to parochial schools, Chief Justice Burger wrote an opinion on behalf of the Court that enunciated a test for determining whether governmental interactions with religion violate the Establishment Clause of the First Amendment.[10] Burger's three-part test for such cases concerning the separation of church and state examined legislators' motivations underlying the creation of the governmental policy, potential favoritism toward particular religions as a consequence of the policy, and any excessive entanglement between government and religion. The Court proceeded to apply the test to invalidate parochial school aid laws, school prayer statutes, and other governmental policies affecting religion.

However, when the Supreme Court was presented with a challenge to the practice of having a Christian minister read prayers at the beginning of each session of the Nebraska State Senate, several justices exhibited collective amnesia by ignoring the test that they had been applying since 1971.[11] The justices in the majority backed away from the prospect of declaring legislative prayer to be unconstitutional, and thus they saved a long-standing practice in Congress as well as in state legislatures. So the justices in the majority ignored the principles that were purported to govern issues concerning separation of church and state in order to make an ad hoc decision that spared them from the fierce public criticism and political backlash that would have inevitably followed a decision to abolish legislative prayer. After approving legislative prayer, the justices returned to using Burger's 1971 test in subsequent cases concerning church and state.

Justice Scalia is unusual among Supreme Court justices because of his persistent efforts to espouse and explain his textualist and originalist approaches to constitutional interpretation through speeches, articles, and judicial opinions. Although he is not completely immune from decision-making inconsistencies, he seems less inclined to make *ad hoc* decisions that appear designed to avoid the prospect of political backlash or to ensure a conservative case outcome.

During the Reagan administration, the perpetual debate about how the Constitution should be interpreted came to the forefront of the legal community because Reagan's attorney general, Edwin Meese, and other officials were exceptionally outspoken in advocating that the justices apply an "original intent" approach in interpreting the Constitution. Political conservatives focused on liberal Justice William Brennan, a member of the Warren Court, as symbolizing an illegitimate approach to constitutional interpretation because Brennan viewed the Constitution as a flexible document that could change in meaning as society evolved. To Brennan, the essential core of the Constitution was American society's pursuit of the ideals of human dignity, so he did not hesitate to interpret the document in ways that expanded civil liberties protections for individuals and curtailed the power of government.[12] By contrast, Meese and other political conservatives viewed the originalist approach to constitutional interpretation as the means to reduce judicial power, undo the liberal judicial decisions of the Warren Court era that they found to be so objectionable, and give more discretionary authority to executive branch officials. According to Meese:

In my opinion a drift back toward the radical egalitarianism and expansive civil libertarianism of the Warren Court would once again be a threat to the notion of limited but energetic government. What, then, should a constitutional jurisprudence actually be? It should be a jurisprudence of original intention.[13]

Meese's advocacy of the originalist theory was relatively easy to criticize because Meese essentially ignored widespread scholarly questions about whether the framers of the Constitution shared specific intentions about the meaning of every provision and, if such intentions existed, whether they are knowable to twentieth-century judges and applicable to twentieth-century legal problems. Archibald Cox, for example, viewed "the genius of the Founding Fathers, . . . [as] in their remarkable capacity for saying enough but . . . not so much as to inhibit their successors who would live in changed and changing worlds."[14]

Meese also blatantly reinterpreted history if it did not comport with the desired ends he sought to justify through originalist theory. For example, he claimed, quite erroneously, that the authors of the Fourteenth Amendment's Equal Protection Clause intended to end school segregation with the ratification of the amendment in 1868, and thus, according to Meese, the Supreme Court's well-accepted decision in *Brown v. Board of Education* really was commanded by original intent.[15] In fact, the members of Congress who initiated the Fourteenth Amendment were responsible for maintaining racial segregation in the Washington, D.C. public schools and congressional visitors' galleries, so the Warren Court had to apply a more flexible interpretation of the Constitution in order to reach its decision in *Brown*.[16]

In contrast to Meese's forceful but careless advocacy of original intent, Justice Scalia presented more thoughtful arguments for the desirability of looking to the framers' intentions as the means to guide contemporary judicial decision making. Like Meese, Scalia advocates originalism in constitutional interpretation to lessen the glaring risk inherent in Brennan's flexible interpretive approach that judges will simply impose their own personal values into their decisions about the Constitution's meaning. According to Scalia, "the main danger in judicial interpretation of the Constitution— or, for that matter, in judicial interpretation of any law—is that the judges will mistake their own predilections for the law."[17] Justice Scalia looked to the framers for guidance because "[o]riginalism does not aggravate the principal weakness of the system, for it establishes a historical criterion that is conceptually quite separate from the preferences of the judge himself [*sic*]."[18]

Scalia differed from Meese, however, in admitting that "originalism . . . is not without its warts. Its greatest defect, in my view, is the difficulty of applying it correctly. . . . a task sometimes better suited to the historian than the lawyer."[19] Moreover, Scalia, unlike Meese, did not cling to originalist theory as a simple "magic wand" that could be waved over every case to produce the correct result. Scalia admitted that in some cases, especially Eighth Amendment cases concerning cruel and unusual punishments, he would apply a flexible interpretation that reflected the evolution of societal values: "I may prove a faint-hearted originalist. I cannot imagine myself, any more than any other federal judge, upholding a statute that imposes the punishment of flogging [which was accepted by the Constitution's authors]."[20] Although some critics might argue that a theory of constitutional interpretation is not much of a theory if you cannot apply it to every situation, Scalia would disagree. For Scalia, originalism provides a useful, if imperfect, approach for reducing the risk that judges will impose their own values in enunciating the meaning of the Constitution.

Justice Scalia is unique among members of the Rehnquist Court in his advocacy of originalism as the appropriate theory of constitutional interpretation. If Robert Bork had gained confirmation in 1987, Scalia would have been joined by the most notable advocate of originalism among contemporary legal scholars. However, Bork was rejected by the Senate, and the other conservatives on the Rehnquist Court were less inclined than Scalia to enunciate comprehensive normative visions of constitutional interpretation. Justice Clarence Thomas agreed with Scalia in nearly 80 percent of the Court's nonunanimous decisions during Thomas's initial term in 1991–92,[21] so Thomas may eventually prove to share Scalia's emphasis on originalism.

Scalia's other closest ally, Chief Justice Rehnquist, who agreed with Scalia in 78 percent of nonunanimous cases in the 1990 term and 74 percent in the 1991 term,[22] specifically disassociated himself from originalism when Attorney General Meese was stirring up a storm of controversy about constitutional interpretation during the Reagan administration.[23] However, Rehnquist, like many other justices, is willing to rely on original intent in specific situations in which the theory will advance his preferred outcomes. For example, in a case concerning the constitutionality of state-sponsored prayer in public schools, Rehnquist dissented against the Court's ban on such prayer by asserting:

The true meaning of the Establishment Clause can only be seen in its history. . . . As drafters of our Bill of Rights, the Framers inscribed the principles that control today. Any deviation from their intentions frustrates the permanence of that Charter and will only lead to the type of unprincipled decision making that has plagued our Establishment Clause cases.[24]

As Rehnquist's words imply, the Chief Justice, like Scalia, feels deep concerns about preventing judges from being "a small group of fortunately situated people with a roving commission to second-guess Congress, state legislatures, and state and federal administrative officers concerning what is best for the country."[25]

Rehnquist and Scalia are two of the most consistently conservative justices on the Rehnquist Court. Rehnquist favored civil liberties claimants in an average of only 22 percent of cases during each term from 1986 to 1990, the lowest percentage on the Court. Scalia favored civil liberties claimants an average of 33 percent during the span, thus tying Justice O'Connor for the honor of being the Court's second-most conservative justice.[26]

Although Rehnquist and Scalia might not always claim to have followed the same general approach to constitutional interpretation, their philosophical affinity and shared concerns about liberal jurisprudence provide them with substantial common ground in interpreting the Constitution. According to Sue Davis's definitive work on Rehnquist's jurisprudence, "Rehnquist's approach includes the belief that the Constitution is limited to the text of the document, the idea that the Constitution has fixed meaning, and the view that it comprises a set of rules to be strictly followed."[27] These principles underlying Chief Justice Rehnquist's judicial decision making are essentially shared by Justice Scalia. Rehnquist places particular emphasis on the importance of fidelity to the words of the Constitution in order to avoid the risk of judges imposing their own values. In Rehnquist's words, "Yet to go beyond the language of the Constitution, and the meaning that may be fairly ascribed to the language, and into the consciences of individual judges, is to embark on a journey that is treacherous indeed."[28] By highlighting the need to follow "the meaning that may be fairly ascribed to the [Constitution's] language," Rehnquist accurately described a central element of Justice Scalia's approach to constitutional interpretation: textualism.

Because Scalia acknowledges the weaknesses of originalism as a comprehensive theory of constitutional interpretation, especially the difficulty in knowing and applying accurately the intentions of eighteenth-century men, he relies on textualism to provide him with another interpretive anchor to diminish the risk of imposing personal values in judicial decision making. In fact, Scalia's reliance on the words of the Constitution provided him with a basis to distinguish himself from Meese and other originalists during his confirmation hearings. Unlike Meese, who advocated fidelity to the original *intentions* of the framers, Scalia believed in following the original *meaning* of the framers' words.[29] Thus, to Scalia, "if somebody should discover that the secret intent of the framers was quite different from what the words connote, it would not make a difference."[30] By relying on the words themselves, which presumably reflect the essence of the framers' intentions, judges can both restrain inclinations to impose personal values on interpretive decisions and avoid potentially fruitless and controversial searches for the precise "true" intentions of a legislative body that met more than 200 years ago.

Although Scalia's opinions may not always be faithful to the interpretive approaches that he espouses, his emphasis on textualism and originalism appears to make him less inclined than his conservative colleagues to rationalize conservative judicial outcomes with ad hoc reasoning. In fact, Scalia's approach led him to join the Court's liberals in a number of opinions supporting individuals' assertions of right against government interference. For example, in several cases concerning the Confrontation Clause, Scalia has joined the most liberal justices and even authored opinions asserting that criminal defendants have a categorical and clearly stated right to confront their accusers, even when child sex abuse victims would be traumatized by facing their alleged abusers in person in the courtroom.[31] Similarly, Scalia joined the Court's liberals and parted company with most of his usual conservative allies in opposing random drug testing of U.S. Customs Service employees[32] and in supporting the right of protestors to burn American flags as a form of protected political expression.[33] Scalia is one of the Rehnquist Court's most consistent conservatives, but the guiding principles underlying his interpretation of the Constitution lead him to disagree with the other conservative justices when he believes that the text of the Constitution dictates a liberal case outcome.

Statutory Interpretation

In statutory interpretation, Scalia has been labeled the leader of the movement toward "the new textualism," which "posits that once the Court has ascertained a statute's plain meaning, consideration of legislative history becomes irrelevant."[34] Although Scalia did not persuade a majority of justices to adopt his views, he gained influence and, simultaneously, forced members of Congress to rethink their approach to creating new statutes. For example, Scalia influenced the development of a crime bill in Congress during 1991:

When the House Judiciary Committee was drafting an anti-crime bill two weeks ago, some members suggested resolving a dispute by putting compromise language into a committee report, which accompanies a bill to the floor. But Barney Frank, D-Mass., warned off his colleagues with just two words: "Justice Scalia."[35]

As in his approach to constitutional interpretation, Scalia's application of textualism to statutes reflects a desire to limit and simplify the judge's task in fulfilling the purposes of legislation. Legislative history underlying a statute can contain speeches and reports with contradictory assertions by partisan legislative opponents endeavoring to have ambiguous statutory language subsequently interpreted to favor their preferred interests. Thus, judges who use legislative history frequently can make many interpretive choices that effectively enable them to use their own values to define a statute's meaning. Scalia's emphasis on defining legislation through the words of the statute, rather than through words in accompanying legislative testimony, speeches, and reports, is consistent with his desire to limit judicial power and the risk that judges will confuse their own preferences with those of the people's elected representatives who authored the legislation.

Scalia's personal crusade to persuade his colleagues to abandon their accustomed practice of examining legislative history in statutory interpretation leads him to seize every opportunity to remind the other justices that he views traditional statutory interpretation as undesirable and a waste of time. Even when Scalia agrees with the other justices on the interpretation of a statutory provision, he writes separate opinions to advocate his approach to statutory interpretation. For example, in a unanimous decision in which the justices all agreed on the meaning of the word *burglary* in a statute, Scalia scored his colleagues for, in his view, their unnecessary reliance on legislative history. His concurring opinion in this relatively minor case illustrates both his commitment to establishing a new approach to statutory interpretation and his outspokenness in criticizing his colleagues, both liberals and conservatives:

I join in the Court's opinion except for Part II, which examines in great detail the statute's legislative history. The examination does not uncover anything useful (*i.e.*, anything that tempts us to alter the meaning we deduce from the text anyway), but that is the usual consequence of these inquiries (and a good thing, too). What is noteworthy, however, is that in this case it is hard to understand what we would have done if we *had* found anything useful. The Court says, correctly, that the statutory term "burglary" has a "generally accepted contemporary meaning" which must be given effect, and which may not be modified by a rule of lenity. . . . But if the meaning is so clear that it cannot be constricted by that venerable canon of construction, surely it is not so ambiguous that it can be constricted by the sundry floor statements, witness testimony, and other legislative incunabula that the Court discusses. Is it conceivable that we look to the legislative history only to determine whether it displays, not a *less* extensive punitive intent than the plain meaning (the domain of the rule of lenity), but a *more* extensive one? If we found a more extensive one, I assume we would then have to apply the rule of lenity, bringing us back once again to the ordinary meaning of the statute. It seems like a lot of trouble. I can discern no reason for devoting ten pages of today's opinion to legislative history, except to show that we have given this case close and careful consideration. We must find some better way of demonstrating our conscientiousness.[36]

Scalia's approach to statutory interpretation involves a change in the "rules of the game" for legislators writing new laws. If Scalia persuades his colleagues to follow his approach, legislators will have to be much more careful about how they draft statutes. This may not be a bad thing if it produces more clarity from legislators about what laws are supposed to mean.

In the interim, however, Scalia's new approach has significant effects on the meaning of laws already written under the "old rules." Because Scalia's judicial philosophy emphasizes both textualism and deference to officials in other branches of government, in disputed cases Scalia opts to defer to the executive branch's interpretation of law as long as that interpretation is reasonable according to the words of the statute. Such outcomes comport with the academic argument most closely associated with Scalia's name when he was a law professor and the editor of *Regulation*, namely "minimiz[ing] judicial control of [executive] agency activity."[37]

Because Scalia's service on the Rehnquist Court from 1986 to 1993 came during Republican presidential administrations, deference to agencies' interpretations also tended to produce outcomes consistent with Scalia's political conservatism. The test of Scalia's consistency and adherence to interpretive theory will come during the Democratic Clinton administration. In the meantime, Scalia's approach can produce significant power shifting from the legislative and judicial branches to the executive branch on particular issues. This alteration of the relationships between the branches of government has generated hostility toward Scalia among some members of Congress.[38]

Separation of Powers

One of Scalia's strongest and most enduring commitments is to a strict conception of separation of powers. As one observer noted, Scalia's "dedication to the doctrine of separation of powers may be his strongest present doctrinal commitment, aside from his rejection of affirmative action."[39] Prior to his appointment to the Supreme Court, Scalia gained notice as an articulate spokesman for the preservation of clear lines of authority between Congress and the executive. In assessing his legal career, Justice Scalia commented that "[i]f there is anyone who, over the years, had a greater interest in the subject of separation of powers, he does not come readily to mind."[40]

As a member of the Ford administration in the mid-1970s, Scalia was the assistant attorney general who testified before Congress in opposition to the "legislative veto," the practice through which an executive agency is given authority by Congress to act with the stipulation that one or both houses of Congress can subsequently overturn the executive action. According to Barbara Craig, "Assistant Attorney General Scalia was a willing knight well prepared to ride into battle. . . . [The] feisty constitutional expert had no doubts in his own mind about the legislative veto's unconstitutionality, and no hesitancy in speaking his mind to anyone who would listen."[41]

In his academic writing as a law professor, Scalia wrote a law review article, described by a legal scholar as "[o]ne of the most influential,"[42] criticizing the legislative veto as a usurpation of executive power by Congress.[43] Subsequently, Scalia authored the American Bar Association (ABA) amicus brief opposing the constitutionality of the legislative veto in *Immigration and Naturalization Service v. Chadha*, the case in which the Supreme Court ultimately struck down the legislative device.[44] Scalia was the driving force behind the ABA's amicus brief, and his "talents as a skilled negotiator were put to their full test as he worked with [another attorney] who was more than a little resistant to attacking the veto as broadly as Scalia wished."[45]

Later, as a judge for the District of Columbia Circuit, Scalia wrote an article that emphasized the importance of separation of powers within the American governing system by highlighting James Madison's well-known pronouncements on the subject. Moreover, he noted that "no less than five of the Federalist Papers were devoted to the demonstration that the principle [of separation of powers] was adequately observed in the proposed Constitution."[46]

While serving as an appellate judge, Scalia sat on the special three-judge district court panel that determined that the Gramm-Rudman-Hollings Balanced Budget and Emergency Deficit Control Act, which automatically operated to cut and balance the federal budget, unconstitutionally infringed on executive power. Scalia was widely rumored to have authored the unsigned, per curiam opinion[47] that was subsequently affirmed by the Supreme Court in *Bowsher v. Synar*.[48] Thus, as an assistant attorney general, law professor, and federal appellate judge, Scalia played an important role in two of the most historic separation of powers cases, *Chadha* and *Bowsher*, both of which were decided by the Supreme Court in accordance with Scalia's restrictive views. After being elevated to the Supreme Court in 1986, however, Scalia became the solitary dissenter in subsequent separation of powers cases.

In *Morrison v. Olson*, the Supreme Court rejected separation of powers claims in order to endorse the use of independent counsels to investigate wrongdoing by executive branch officials.[49] In *Mistretta v. United States*, the Supreme Court approved the use of a U.S. Sentencing Commission, composed of representatives from, or appointed by, all three branches of government, with responsibility for developing sentencing guidelines to be applied to punish offenders who violate federal criminal laws.[50] The other justices on the Supreme Court appeared to move toward a flexible, pragmatic conception of separation of powers that permitted the use of new innovations to deal with intractable problems, even if those innovations blurred the lines of authority between the branches of government. Scalia, by contrast, was the solitary dissenter who continued to argue forcefully for a rigid conception of separation of powers.

Justice Scalia's persistent interest in separation of powers is indicative of the importance that he attributes to the issue. Fundamentally, Scalia sees individuals' personal rights and liberties as resting on the preservation of clearly divided authority between the branches of government. As Scalia explained in a televised panel discussion:

The public generally, law students, and, I am sorry to say, most lawyers regard separation of powers as dealing with a hyper-technical picky-picky portion of the Constitution. Of concern to politicians, perhaps, but of no real interest to the people. What the people care about, what affects them, is the Bill of Rights. . . . That is a *profoundly* mistaken view. . . . For the fact is, that it is the structure of government, its constitution, in the real sense of that word, that ultimately preserves or destroys freedom. The Bill of Rights is no more than ink on paper unless . . . it is addressed to a government which is so constituted that no part of it can obtain excessive power.[51]

From Scalia's perspective, any deviation, no matter how minor or apparently inconsequential, from the strict boundaries that separate the authority and functions of the respective branches of government may ultimately lead to the excessive accumulation of power in a single branch and thereby threaten individual liberty.

Justice Scalia is fond of comparing the many specific, and historically unfulfilled, individual rights guaranteed in the constitution of the old Soviet Union with the limited but effective rights contained in the American Bill of Rights in order to demonstrate that separated power within the governing structure rather than explicit constitutional guarantees actually ensures individual liberty. As Scalia wrote in his *Morrison* dissent, "Without a secure structure of separated powers, our Bill of Rights would be worthless, as are the bills of rights of many nations of the world that have adopted, or even improved upon, the mere words of ours."[52] Scalia also emphasizes the fact that the original Constitution did not even contain a Bill of Rights to show that the framers felt that the structure of government provided the most important protection for individuals' rights. As indicated by his solitary dissents in *Morrison* and *Mistretta*, Scalia did not convince any of his colleagues that rigid separation of powers is essential to the maintenance of liberty in American society.

Reducing the Federal Courts' Caseload

One means to reduce judicial involvement in issues that, in Scalia's eyes, are appropriately left under the authority of the legislative and executive branches of government is to keep cases from being reviewed by federal judges. Scalia has taken several approaches to advance his goal of reducing the number of cases brought before the federal courts.

As an appellate judge, Scalia was a strong advocate of narrowly applying the doctrine of standing when considering whether a claimant could properly initiate a claim in the federal courts. A person has "standing" to initiate litigation when the judicial system recognizes him or her (or a group) as being the proper, injured party entitled to seek judicial assistance in a dispute. Many of the most significant questions related to standing concern situations in which an interest group wants to initiate a lawsuit in order to pursue its policy objectives. For example, can an environmental group file an action to prevent a historic redwood tree from being cut down? Can that group show that it will be sufficiently harmed by the tree's removal to justify the group's participation in a lawsuit?

In pursuing his objective of keeping cases out of the courts, Scalia has frequently sought to limit the recognition that litigants have standing to initiate cases. He authored an article that argued that strict application of standing was an essential element underlying separation of powers (another of Scalia's favorite concerns) as a means to prevent judicial interference with other branches of government.[53] If courts do not entertain arguments from claimants seeking to challenge governmental policies, then the judiciary will not be tempted to interfere with the work of the other branches of government. Analyses of Scalia's work as an appellate judge always emphasize Scalia's repeated efforts to use the doctrine of standing as a means to limit the number of cases brought into the federal court system.[54] According to one scholar, Judge Scalia was "particularly adept at invoking procedural defenses to constitutional claims. . . . [H]e ruled against sixteen out of seventeen civil plaintiffs who claimed their constitutional rights had been violated. He decided twelve of those cases on procedural grounds."[55]

In his first major address to the ABA after being appointed to the Supreme Court, Justice Scalia expressed concern about the "continuing deterioration" of the prestige of the federal courts.[56] According to Scalia, the framers of the Constitution intended for the federal judiciary to be a "natural aristocracy . . . of ability rather than wealth,"[57] but the federal courts have lost their elite status because they are overloaded with too many cases, including routine cases that do not need to be heard by federal judges. Scalia believes that appointing additional judges to handle the caseload would not solve the problem because an increase in the number of federal judges merely dilutes the prestige of judicial office. Scalia also rejects the idea of an "Intercircuit Tribunal," a new appellate court below the Supreme Court to ease some of the high court's burden, because such a new court would only exacerbate current problems by inviting lawyers to continue to file burdensome appeals. Instead, Scalia advocates reducing both the number and kinds of cases permitted to be filed in federal courts.

As a Supreme Court justice, Scalia has joined numerous opinions that advocated restricted access to the courts for individuals seeking to assert constitutional claims. For example, the conservative majority on the Rehnquist Court, including Scalia, has created new limitations that block federal judicial review for convicted criminal offenders' habeas corpus petitions. *Penry v. Lynaugh*[58] "significantly narrowed the scope of federal habeas by excluding claims based on 'new constitutional rules of civil procedure,' or rules that are announced after a defendant's conviction becomes 'final.' "[59] *McCleskey v. Zant*[60] created a new requirement that prisoners file all of their claims in their first petition, even if government officials have hidden evidence from them for years that would have shown the existence of other constitutional violations. *Coleman v. Thompson*[61] barred federal court review of cases in which the claimant's lawyer violated any state court procedural rules. Other cases limited the retroactive application of Supreme Court decisions[62] and declined to grant death row inmates a right to legal assistance for postconviction litigation.[63] Scalia has gone even further than most of his allies by joining Justice O'Connor to argue that all *Miranda* claims should be barred from the federal courts if they have previously been reviewed in state courts.[64]

In addition, in 1991, when Chief Justice Rehnquist replaced Justice White with Justice Scalia as the circuit justice for the Fifth Circuit Court of Appeals covering Texas, Louisiana, and Mississippi, a circuit that produces a disproportionate number of the nation's capital punishment cases, Scalia immediately announced he was changing White's policy of granting extensions to death row inmates who were not represented by attorneys.[65] Scalia began to strictly apply the filing deadlines for claims from death row inmates, even though many indigent prisoners are incapable of discovering and following legal procedural rules for pursuing constitutional claims.

The conservative justices, including Scalia, moved ahead with their policy objective of reducing caseload burdens and opportunities for judicial decision making. This effort came at the expense of accessible, thorough federal court reviews of many kinds of constitutional claims, especially those from criminal defendants. As a consequence, the conservative justices' initiative reduced the federal judiciary's responsibility for preventing injustice in individual cases. Because limitations on federal reviews of state criminal convictions increase the likelihood that state courts will make mistakes, the conservative justices' approach ensures that errors will not be corrected by the federal judges who were previously available to review habeas petitions. This shift in emphasis comports with Chief Justice Rehnquist's view that the Supreme Court should not concern itself with correcting injustices. According to Rehnquist, "The Supreme Court of the United States should be reserved . . . for important disputes and questions of law, not for individual injustices that might be corrected and should be corrected in other courts."[66]

As indicated by his efforts to limit access to the federal courts, especially for individuals' claims concerning constitutional rights, Scalia apparently shares Rehnquist's view. In fact, Scalia is regarded as having a "majoritarian vision . . . [that is] skeptical of Earl Warren's faith in a people governing themselves through a conflict encouraged by the existence of rights for [political] minorities."[67] Thus, Justice Scalia has been subjected to criticism because his "broad deference [to state courts and other branches of government] would remove the [federal courts] as a 'shield' and relegate protection of the minority to the unrestrained, and often indifferent, processes of majority rule."[68]

SCALIA'S INFLUENTIAL OPINIONS

The central themes that shape Scalia's decision making manifest themselves in his judicial opinions as well as in his speeches and articles. The strength of Scalia's belief in the rightness of his views is evident in the number of judicial opinions that he produces. He is one of the most prolific writers on the Rehnquist Court. During the 1990 and 1991 terms, for example, Scalia averaged nearly forty-two opinions per term—a figure well above the average of twenty-nine for all of the justices and second only to Justice Stevens's individual average of forty-six opinions per term.[69]

Because Justice Stevens averaged twenty-five dissenting opinions during each of these terms, it is apparent that his productivity is motivated by his role as one of the most liberal justices on the Rehnquist Court who finds himself articulating his disagreements with the dominant conservative majority. By contrast, Scalia is unique in producing concurring opinions. His average of nearly seventeen per term far exceeds the average for all justices (six) and is double the number (eight) produced by his closest competitors in producing concurrences, Stevens and Kennedy.[70] Scalia frequently agrees with the outcomes produced by the Rehnquist Court's conservative majority, but he feels compelled to express his own reasoning as a means to advance his strongly held views on textualism, originalism, and other elements of his judicial philosophy.

A few opinions stand out as examples of the power of Scalia's mind and pen. When Scalia has been able to gather support from a majority of justices, he has been exceptionally influential in shaping constitutional law. In the following exemplary cases, Scalia not only managed to gain the support of a majority on the Court, but he also managed to produce on the Court's behalf controversial opinions that immediately and dramatically changed the state of constitutional law. These were cases in which commentators were not especially surprised by the outcomes because of the conservatives' dominance on the Rehnquist Court. The notable aspects of these cases emerged in Scalia's reasoning that produced sudden, unexpected changes in the definition of individuals' rights under the Bill of Rights.

In regard to the Free Exercise Clause, Scalia wrote the Court's opinion in *Employment Division of Oregon v. Smith*,[71] a case in which the majority rejected Native Americans' claims for unemployment compensation after they lost their jobs because of their sacramental use of peyote as a traditional religious practice. Consistent with his desire to defer whenever possible to the actions of the legislative and executive branches of government, Scalia's opinion significantly narrowed the scope of individuals' free exercise rights.

Guided by Justice Harlan Stone's famous "Footnote Four,"[72] since 1938 the Supreme Court has "view[ed] with a suspicious eye legislative and executive experimentation with . . . basic human freedoms generally regarded as the 'cultural freedoms' guaranteed by the Bill of Rights."[73] The Supreme Court's path-breaking 1963 free exercise decision, *Sherbert v. Verner*,[74] regarding unemployment compensation for Sabbatarians, initiated, as Justice Scalia acknowledged, "the *Sherbert* test [in which] governmental actions that substantially burden a religious practice must be justified by a compelling governmental interest."[75] Although the Native Americans in the *Smith* case asked that Oregon be required to show a compelling state interest to justify its criminal proscription of centuries-old religious use of peyote, Scalia presented the novel argument that the "compelling interest" test only applies to free exercise claims by Sabbatarians seeking unemployment compensation.[76] Scalia further argued that the important precedents in which the Supreme Court had scrutinized and invalidated governmental actions because they infringed on free exercise rights were not actually about the Free Exercise Clause but instead were "hybrid situation[s]" in which free exercise claims were combined with other asserted fundamental rights.[77] Scalia thus reinterpreted, rather than reversed, the prior precedents that stood in the way of his decision to defer to the state government. In spite of the prior precedents to the contrary, Scalia ultimately ruled against the Native Americans by asserting that free exercise claims, other than those concerning Sabbatarians' unemployment compensation, cannot overcome otherwise valid state laws.

Scalia's characterization of classic free exercise cases such as *Cantwell v. Connecticut*[78] and *Wisconsin v. Yoder*[79] as, in effect, not entirely about free exercise flies in the face of standard presentations in constitutional law textbooks. For example, a typical textbook's description of *Cantwell* is as follows: "[The Supreme Court] upheld the right of a Jehovah's Witness who had been prosecuted for violating a state law that prohibited the solicitation of money. . . . A unanimous Court struck down the state law as a violation of the free exercise of religion."[80] *Wisconsin v. Yoder* is described as "the case of members of the Amish religious order who had been convicted for violating Wisconsin's requirement that children attend school until age 16. . . . The Court found that the religious interests of the Amish outweighed the interests of the state."[81]

As might be expected, Scalia's surprising characterization of prior precedents attracted strong rebukes in the opinions of Justices O'Connor and Blackmun, who were joined by Justices Brennan and Marshall. According to O'Connor, "The Court endeavors to escape from our decisions in *Cantwell* and *Yoder* by labeling them 'hybrid' decisions . . . but there is no denying that both cases expressly relied on the Free Exercise Clause . . . and that we have consistently regarded those cases as part of the mainstream of our free exercise jurisprudence."[82] Blackmun reiterated O'Connor's criticism:

This Court over the years painstakingly has developed a consistent and exacting standard to test the constitutionality of a state statute that burdens the free exercise of religion. Such a statute may stand only if the law in general, and the State's refusal to allow a religious exemption in particular, are justified by a compelling interest that cannot be served by less restrictive means. . . .

Until today, I thought this was a settled and inviolate principle of this Court's First Amendment jurisprudence. . . . [T]he majority is able to arrive at this view only by mischaracterizing this Court's precedents. The Court discards leading free exercise cases such as *Cantwell v. Connecticut* . . . and *Wisconsin v. Yoder* . . . as "hybrid."[83]

In spite of the criticism, because Scalia's opinion garnered the support of a majority of justices (i.e., Rehnquist, Kennedy, White, and Stevens), it served as the basis for a sudden, significant change in free exercise jurisprudence. In a single deft opinion, without overruling any prior precedents, Scalia managed to rewrite the generally accepted understanding of constitutional law concerning the free exercise of religion.

In the area of criminal justice, Scalia authored the majority opinion in *Wilson v. Seiter*,[84] which drastically changed the judicial standard of review for prisoners' civil rights cases. In cases challenging conditions of confinement in correctional institutions as violative of the Eighth Amendment, the Supreme Court initially endorsed judicial intervention when an examination of the "totality of conditions" revealed "wanton and unnecessary infliction of pain" or "unquestioned and serious deprivation of basic human needs."[85] In other words, judges were to apply an *objective* standard and order remedies if prison conditions did not meet the standards of the Eighth Amendment.

In the 1991 decision in *Wilson v. Seiter*, however, Scalia's opinion indicated that cases challenging conditions of confinement were to receive judicial remedies only when there was "deliberate indifference" on the part of corrections officials. Thus, the courts no longer look at the conditions of confinement *objectively* to determine if they meet Eighth Amendment standards. Instead, federal judges *subjectively* examine the state of mind of corrections officials to determine if remedies are appropriate.

As a result of this drastic change in standards, Justice White warned that it may be possible for a prison with conditions unfit for human habitation to avoid judicial intervention and remedial action if the correctional administrator merely says, "We are aware and concerned about the conditions, but we simply do not have enough money to correct the problems"—thus no "deliberate indifference."[86]

In this case, the justices unanimously agreed on the outcome, but Scalia was able to get only four other justices to join his opinion. In the Supreme Court, because five votes are enough to set a new precedent, Scalia again managed to rewrite dramatically the state of constitutional law in a single, far-reaching opinion.

In *Harmelin v. Michigan*,[87] Scalia's majority opinion declared that Michigan's law mandating a life sentence without possibility of parole for carrying more than 650 grams of cocaine did not violate the Eighth Amendment. The four dissenters (White, Blackmun, Marshall, and Stevens) complained that Scalia's analysis obliterated the proportionality requirement that had previously been considered part of the Eighth Amendment and therefore, according to Justice White's dissent, Scalia's reasoning would endorse a state's decision to mandate life imprisonment for parking tickets.[88] Unless the proportionality requirement of the Eighth Amendment is clarified in subsequent cases, Scalia's opinion may encourage states to punish all crimes in nearly any manner that they wish, despite the fact that fewer than five justices endorsed Scalia's detailed analytical sections concerning proportionality. Some of Scalia's fellow conservatives agreed with his conclusion about the appropriate case outcome but they expressed misgivings about the dramatic implications of his analysis.

CONCLUSION

Antonin Scalia is a notable member of the Rehnquist Court whose conservative jurisprudence reflects a particular set of interpretive approaches and priorities. Scalia draws upon his judicial philosophy and his goals for the judicial branch to advance his vision of a restrained judiciary reducing its interference with the decisions and actions of the elected officials, both legislative and executive, who represent majoritarian interests in society. Scalia stands out among the conservative justices as one who is clear-sighted in his vision of the Supreme Court's role and whose outspokenness and articulate opinions enable him to influence the shape of constitutional law significantly.

NOTES

1. George Kannar, "The Constitutional Catechism of Antonin Scalia," *Yale Law Journal* 99 (1990): 1308 n. 53.
2. Richard A. Brisbin, Jr., "The Conservatism of Antonin Scalia," *Political Science Quarterly* 105 (1990): 1–2.
3. Antonin Scalia, "The Disease as Cure," *Washington University Law Quarterly* (1979): 147.
4. Lawrence Baum, *The Supreme Court*, 4th ed. (Washington, D.C.: Congressional Quarterly Press, 1992), p. 165.
5. Linda Greenhouse, "Supreme Court Dissenters: Loners or Pioneers?" *New York Times*, 20 July 1991, p. B7.
6. Brisbin, p. 29.
7. Christopher E. Smith, "The Supreme Court and Ethnicity," *Oregon Law Review* 69 (1990): 823–826.
8. Christopher E. Smith and Avis Alexandria Jones, "The Rehnquist Court's Activism and the Risk of Injustice," *Connecticut Law Review* (forthcoming, Fall 1993).
9. Kannar, p. 1301 n. 11.
10. Lemon v. Kurtzman, 403 U.S. 602 (1971).
11. Marsh v. Chambers, 463 U.S. 783 (1983).
12. William Brennan, "The Constitution of the United States: Contemporary Ratification," speech presented at Georgetown University, 12 October 1985, pp. 4–5.
13. Edwin Meese, speech before the American Bar Association House of Delegates, July 1985, quoted in Debra Cassens Moss, "The Policy and the Rhetoric of Ed Meese," *American Bar Association Journal*, 73 (1 February 1987): 66.
14. Archibald Cox, *The Court and the Constitution* (Boston: Houghton Mifflin, 1987), p. 42.
15. Edwin Meese, "The Battle for the Constitution," *Policy Review* 35 (Spring 1986): 34.
16. Christopher E. Smith, "Jurisprudential Politics and the Manipulation of History," *Western Journal of Black Studies* 13 (1989): 156–161.
17. Antonin Scalia, "Originalism: The Lesser Evil," *University of Cincinnati Law Review* 57 (1989): 863.
18. Ibid., p. 864.
19. Ibid., pp. 856–857.
20. Ibid., p. 864.

21. Christopher E. Smith and Scott Patrick Johnson, "The First-Term Performance of Justice Clarence Thomas," *Judicature* 76 (1993): 174.

22. Scott P. Johnson and Christopher E. Smith, "David Souter's First Term on the Supreme Court: The Impact of a New Justice," *Judicature* 75 (1992): 239; Smith and Johnson, "The First-Term Performance," p. 174.

23. "Rehnquist's Perspective," *American Bar Association Journal*, 73 (1 April 1987): 19.

24. Wallace v. Jaffrey, 472 U.S. 38, 113 (1985) (Rehnquist, J., dissenting).

25. William Rehnquist, "The Notion of a Living Constitution," *Texas Law Review* 54 (1976): 698–699.

26. Sheldon Goldman, *Constitutional Law: Cases and Essays*, 2nd ed. (New York: HarperCollins, 1991), p. 150.

27. Sue Davis, *Justice Rehnquist and the Constitution* (Princeton, N.J.: Princeton University Press, 1989), p. 28.

28. William Rehnquist, *The Supreme Court—How It Was; How It Is* (New York: William Morrow, 1987), p. 317.

29. Kannar, p. 1307.

30. Ibid.

31. Cruz v. New York, 481 U.S. 186 (1987); Coy v. Iowa, 487 U.S. 1012 (1988); Maryland v. Craig, 110 S. Ct. 3157, 3171 (1990) (Scalia, J., dissenting).

32. National Treasury Employees Union v. Von Raab, 489 U.S. 656 (1989).

33. Texas v. Johnson, 109 S. Ct. 2533 (1989); United States v. Eichman, 110 S. Ct. 2404 (1990).

34. William N. Eskridge, Jr., "The New Textualism," *U.C.L.A. Law Review* 37 (1990): 623.

35. "Congress Keeps Eye on Justices as Court Watches Hill's Words," *Congressional Quarterly Weekly Report* 49 (1991): 2863.

36. Taylor v. United States, 110 S. Ct. 2143, 2160–2161 (1990) (Scalia, J., concurring).

37. Brisbin, p. 12.

38. David Kaplan and Bob Cohn, "The Court's Mr. Right," *Newsweek*, 5 November 1990, p. 67.

39. Michael King, "Justice Antonin Scalia: The First Term on the Supreme Court—1986–1987," *Rutgers Law Journal* 20 (1988): 67.

40. Remarks of Justice Antonin Scalia at Washington, D.C. Panel Discussion on Separation of Powers (audiotape of C-SPAN broadcast, 15 November 1988).

41. Barbara Craig, *Chadha: The Story of an Epic Constitutional Struggle* (New York: Oxford University Press, 1988), p. 53.

42. James G. Wilson, "Constraints of Power: The Constitutional Opinions of Judges Scalia, Bork, Posner, Easterbrook and Winter," *University of Miami Law Review* 40 (1986): 1200.

43. Antonin Scalia, "The Legislative Veto: A False Remedy for System Overload," *Regulation* 3 (November–December 1979): 19.

44. Immigration and Naturalization Service v. Chadha, 462 U.S. 919 (1983).

45. Craig, p. 186.

46. Antonin Scalia, "The Doctrine of Standing as an Essential Element of the Separation of Powers," *Suffolk University Law Review* 17 (1983): 881.

47. Wilson, p. 1201.

48. Synar v. United States, 676 F. Supp. 1374 (D.D.C.) (per curiam), *aff'd sub nom.* Bowsher v. Synar, 478 U.S. 714 (1986).

49. Morrison v. Olson, 108 S. Ct. 2597 (1988).

50. Mistretta v. United States, 109 S. Ct. 647 (1989).

51. Remarks of Justice Antonin Scalia, 15 November 1988, supra n. 40.

52. Morrison v. Olson, 108 S. Ct. 2597, 2622 (1988) (Scalia, J., dissenting).

53. Scalia, "The Doctrine of Standing," pp. 881–899.

54. Jean Morgan Meaux, "Justice Antonin Scalia and Judicial Restraint: A Conservative Resolution of Conflict between Individual and State," *Tulane Law Review* 62 (1987): 233–237; Richard Nagareda, "The Appellate Jurisprudence of Justice Antonin Scalia," *University of Chicago Law Review* 54 (1987): 706–715.

55. Wilson, p. 1181.

56. Stuart Taylor, "Scalia Proposes Major Overhaul of U.S. Courts," *New York Times*, 16 February 1987, p. 1.

57. Ibid.

58. Penry v. Lynaugh, 109 S. Ct. 2934 (1989).

59. Joseph L. Hoffmann, "The Supreme Court's New Vision of Federal Habeas Corpus for State Prisoners," *Supreme Court Review* (1989): 166.

60. McCleskey v. Zant, 111 S. Ct. 1454 (1991).

61. Coleman v. Thompson, 111 S. Ct. 2546 (1991).

62. Butler v. McKellar, 110 S. Ct. 1212 (1990).

63. Murray v. Giarratano, 109 S. Ct. 2765 (1989).

64. Duckworth v. Eagan, 109 S. Ct. 2875 (1989).

65. Linda Greenhouse, "Scalia Tightens Policy on Death Penalty Appeals," *New York Times*, 22 February 1991, p. B16.

66. William H. Rehnquist, PBS documentary film, *This Honorable Court: Inside the Marble Temple*, broadcast on 12 September 1989.

67. Brisbin, p. 29.

68. Meaux, p. 257.

69. Christopher E. Smith, "Justice Antonin Scalia and Criminal Justice Cases," *Kentucky Law Journal* 81 (1992–93): 195.

70. Ibid.

71. Employment Division of Oregon v. Smith, 110 S. Ct. 1595 (1990).

72. United States v. Carolene Products Co., 304 U.S. 144, 153 n. 4 (1938).

73. Henry J. Abraham, *Freedom and the Court*, 5th ed. (New York: Oxford University Press, 1988), p. 18.

74. Sherbert v. Verner, 374 U.S. 398 (1963).

75. Employment Division of Oregon v. Smith, 110 S. Ct. 1595, 1602 (1990).

76. Ibid.

77. Ibid., pp. 1601–1602.

78. Cantwell v. Connecticut, 310 U.S. 296 (1940).

79. Wisconsin v. Yoder, 406 U.S. 205 (1972).

80. Louis Fisher, *American Constitutional Law* (New York: McGraw-Hill, 1990), p. 705.

81. Ibid., p. 706.

82. Employment Division of Oregon v. Smith, 110 S. Ct. 1595, 1609 (1990) (O'Connor, J., concurring in the judgment).

83. Employment Division of Oregon v. Smith, 110 S. Ct. 1595, 1615–1616 (1990) (Blackmun, J., dissenting).

84. Wilson v. Seiter, 111 S. Ct. 2321 (1991).

85. Rhodes v. Chapman, 452 U.S. 337, 347 (1981).

86. Wilson v. Seiter, 111 S. Ct. 2321, 2330 (1991) (White, J., concurring in judgment).

87. Harmelin v. Michigan, 111 S. Ct. 2680 (1991).

88. Ibid., p. 2709 (White, J., dissenting).

Justice Scalia's Judicial Behavior

As indicated by the previous chapter's overview of Justice Scalia's judicial philosophy and influence on constitutional jurisprudence, he has earned a reputation for being a brilliant, outspoken, and influential proponent of clearly defined ideas. Although Scalia has not always persuaded other justices to agree with his reasoning, his opinions usually produce the same outcomes favored by the Rehnquist Court's conservative majority. Why, then, has Scalia been unable to achieve his vision? Why have the conservatives been unwilling or unable to act in concert in reversing the Warren Court's judicial role and doctrines that political conservatives find so objectionable? In large part, the answers to these questions can be found by examining other aspects of Justice Scalia's judicial behavior that detract from his ability to influence his like-minded colleagues consistently and effectively.

DECISION MAKING IN THE SUPREME COURT

The stereotypical image of decision making in courts, including the Supreme Court, portrays judicial officers as wise and learned experts on legal matters who answer the questions presented to them by finding and applying "the law." To the extent that this image implies that judicial officers always find existing answers buried within the dusty law books that fill the shelves of law libraries, this image is incorrect and deceiving. It is true that lower court judges must frequently obey the case decisions of higher courts in order to avoid having their decisions reversed. It is also true that higher appellate courts, including the Supreme Court, often use precedents established in previous cases to guide their reasoning and decisions. It is not true, however, that Supreme Court justices "find" the law. Much of the time there is no law to find, and they must simply create new rules for society through their authority to interpret statutes and the U.S. Constitution. In other cases, the justices use their interpretive powers to change the existing case law as, for example, when the Warren Court justices suddenly declared school segregation unconstitutional in 1954 many years after their predecessors in 1896 had approved such practices in a long-standing precedent.

Chief Justice Rehnquist has admitted that "[t]here simply is no demonstrably 'right' answer to the question involved in many of our difficult cases."[1] Thus, as a practical matter, the meaning of constitutional law at any given moment in history is whatever five justices of the Supreme Court say it is. This notion that the law's meaning is in the hands of mere human beings who happen to be wearing black robes may offend society's assumptions about the enduring principles of law and the deserved reverence for courts as legal rather than political institutions. However, the cold reality is that constitutional law is quite malleable, depending on the political composition of the Supreme Court and the inclinations of individual justices. Specific constitutional principles may become permanent if justices agree with them generation after generation or if later justices believe that stability in society precludes changing them. Other principles may change very quickly if the Court's composition changes or if justices on the Court change their minds about how an issue should be decided. In 1940, for example, the Supreme Court ruled, eight to one, that children who were Jehovah's Witnesses could be expelled from school for refusing to salute the American flag.[2] By 1943, three justices had changed their minds on the issue and new justices with different views had been appointed to the Court, so that the high court reversed itself in a six-to-three decision and recognized the right of Jehovah's Witnesses to exercise their religious beliefs freely by declining to salute.[3]

Because constitutional law does not consist of fixed principles and can change according to the decisions of the Supreme Court, individual justices must gain the support of at least four other colleagues in order to produce opinions that change or reinforce constitutional law. Unless the Court is filled with like-minded justices, frequently it is not sufficient for a justice to say, "Here is what I think about the issue." In order to advance their preferred case outcomes and constitutional principles, justices must engage in strategic behavior that will increase the likelihood that a majority of justices will support their position.

Scholars have analyzed justices' strategic behavior based on the papers of retired justices and information from law clerks and, occasionally, the justices themselves.[4] Walter Murphy's classic study, for example, showed how justices attempt to persuade, flatter, bargain, and otherwise engage in strategic behavior to influence their colleagues' decisions.[5] Scholars have also studied chief justices' leadership styles,[6] the impact of interpersonal conflict between individual justices,[7] and other factors that shape the formation of majority coalitions within the Court concerning specific issues.[8] Because no two justices share precisely the same views on all issues, the effectiveness of justices in advancing their preferred principles and outcomes depends not only on the number of like-minded colleagues they have on the Court but also on their strategic behavior in persuading colleagues to join their opinions. Justice William Brennan, for example, had a reputation as an effective politician within the Court who understood his various colleagues' attitudes and feelings and who could shape opinions to attract needed support.[9]

Strategic interactions between justices are not visible to scholars because the justices keep the Supreme Court shrouded in a cloak of secrecy. The justices seek to protect the high court's image and legitimacy by discussing and voting on their decisions in secret conferences attended only by the justices themselves. In order to increase the likelihood that the American public will respect and obey the Supreme Court's decisions, the justices' elaborate opinions justify their case decisions with legal arguments and terminology. They do not describe the discussions that took place when the case was being decided. Because the justices believe, perhaps with good reason, that their effectiveness depends on the public's faith in the legal basis of their decisions, they traditionally attempt to hide from public view the political interactions that shape many case outcomes.[10] Despite the Court's inaccessibility to scholars, strategic behavior by justices is often discernible in the justices' published opinions. By seeing the formation and changes in Court majorities concerning specific issues as well as the reasoning in opinions associated with those changes, the justices' strategic behaviors are detectable.

In *Enmund v. Florida*,[11] for example, the driver of a getaway car was sentenced to death under the felony murder rule for a homicide committed by his accomplices during a robbery. Because there was no evidence of his participation in the actual killing, a slim five-member majority on the Supreme Court disallowed the death sentence in an opinion by Justice Byron White. The majority's opinion required prosecutors to show, and juries to find, a clear and immediate link between the defendant's actions and the death of the homicide victim. Justice White wrote:

For purposes of imposing the death penalty, Enmund's criminal culpability must be limited to his participation in the robbery, and his punishment must be tailored to his personal responsibility and moral guilt. Putting Enmund to death to avenge two killings that he did not commit and had no intention of committing or causing does not measurably contribute to the retributive end of ensuring that the criminal gets his just deserts.[12]

Justice Sandra O'Connor wrote a vigorous dissent on behalf of the four dissenters who objected to the new rule limiting the death penalty to people who actively participate in unlawful killings.

A few years later, Justice O'Connor wrote an opinion (*Tison v. Arizona*)[13] for a slim five-member majority that, contrary to the rule in *Enmund*, approved the death penalty for two young men who helped their father escape from prison and accompanied him on the escape, during the course of which the father brutally murdered four people. Although O'Connor objected vigorously to the *Enmund* decision, her *Tison* opinion purported to accept *Enmund* as established precedent but then proceeded to create an ambiguous rule approving the execution of accomplices who show "reckless disregard for human life"[14] even if they do not participate in the actual killing. Instead of having a clear link between the defendant's action and the homicide as the basis for the death penalty, O'Connor's rule permits prosecutors, judges, and juries to use their discretion to impose capital punishment on accomplices. Why did O'Connor not directly reverse *Enmund* instead of subverting the *Enmund* rule in a subtle fashion? It was obvious from her original dissenting opinion that she thought *Enmund* was wrongly decided, yet she made no mention of her opposition to the *Enmund* decision.

O'Connor's opinion was written strategically in order to gain the necessary votes to achieve her preferred outcome of permitting states to execute accomplices in felony cases that result in homicides. O'Connor and the *Enmund* dissenters needed to find a fifth vote to create a new majority in order to resume death sentences for accomplices who do not participate directly in homicides. Because four justices from the

Enmund majority (Brennan, Marshall, Blackmun, and Stevens) were strongly opposed to permitting the execution of felony accomplices who do not actually participate in killings, the only justice available for persuasion turned out to be Justice White, a Democratic appointee who tends to be conservative on criminal justice issues. If O'Connor attempted to reverse the *Enmund* decision outright in her opinion, she would have been less likely to attract Justice White. In order to gain a reversal of *Enmund*, White would have been forced to admit that the rule he himself created in *Enmund* was erroneous. Rather than force White to repudiate his own work, O'Connor attracted him to the new majority by purporting to support *Enmund* while actually subtly erasing its effect through the creation of the ambiguous standard in *Tison*. As illustrated by this example, the opinion-writing process provides opportunities for justices to change, ignore, recharacterize, and abolish precedents in a strategic manner in order to appeal to the interests of specific colleagues whom they wish to attract to their majority coalition for a specific case.

JUSTICE SCALIA AS THE ANTISTRATEGIST

As indicated by the foregoing discussion of justices' strategic behavior, the Supreme Court's decision-making process, unlike that of a trial court with a single judge acting alone, requires collegiality. Although the justices work independently in drafting and circulating opinions, the justices must maintain good relationships with each other in order to discuss opinions and form stable majorities as they decide complex cases. According to Lawrence Baum:

[T]here is . . . a critical group element to the Court's decision making. Part of the decisional process occurs in the group settings of oral argument and the Court's conferences. Further, the justices have incentives to interact and work together on decisions outside of conference. The shared goal of seeking majority approval for an opinion in each case often requires interaction. The desire to obtain as much consensus as possible gives justices further reason to work together to reach agreement on outcomes and opinions.[15]

Despite the widespread recognition of the strategic and interactive processes that produce Supreme Court decisions, Justice Scalia appears to be constitutionally incapable of participating in the collegial decision-making process in a manner that will maximize his effectiveness. As described in Chapter 2, Scalia has strongly held views about the proper approach to constitutional and statutory interpretation—views that sometimes clash with those of his usual allies among the Court's conservatives. In addition, the strength of Scalia's belief in the rightness of his views and his professorial style of lecturing his colleagues diminish his ability to participate effectively in the Court's interactive process. If Scalia merely disagreed with his colleagues about specific cases, he might be able to persuade justices about other issues and otherwise perform effectively within the Court's collegial decision-making environment. However, the tone of Scalia's opinions and his style as a participant in the Court's decision-making processes have reduced his effectiveness by actually deterring like-minded colleagues from joining his opinions.

Scalia's Strident Opinions

Justice Scalia joined the Supreme Court in 1986 with a reputation as an outspoken conservative. He was known to state his views with an assertiveness and stridency indicative of a man who lacks any self-doubt about the correctness of his views. Although he was also known as a friendly and likeable person, his penchant for stating his views in the strongest possible terms, both before and after becoming an associate justice, created a recipe for friction within the human, interactive decision-making processes of the Supreme Court.

For example, as a law professor, Scalia wrote an article that both condemned Justice Lewis Powell's carefully crafted opinion on affirmative action[16] and belittled it with sarcasm. Scalia blasted Powell's opinion as "an [*sic*] historic trivialization of the Constitution" and "an embarrassment to teach."[17] He proceeded to ridicule Powell's opinion by sarcastically proposing a "Restorative Justice Handicapping System" for awarding points to various ethnic groups based on their degree of victimization.[18] Scalia went even further by implicitly comparing affirmative action, as approved by Powell and other justices on the Supreme Court, with actions by Adolf Hitler's Nazi Germany:

[W]hat was good enough for Nazi Germany is not good enough for our purposes. We must further divide the Aryans into subgroups. . . . It will, to be sure, be difficult drawing precise lines and establishing the correct number of handicapping points, but having reviewed the Supreme Court's jurisprudence on abortion, I am convinced that our Justices would not shrink from the task.[19]

Such odious comparisons are certain to offend, especially when directed at justices who, unlike Scalia, were adults during World War II and therefore remember very well the crimes perpetrated by the Nazis. When Scalia wrote this article in 1979 with a Democratic president occupying the White House, he had no way of knowing that he would be appointed to the Supreme Court a few short years later. Thus, the article written in his capacity as a law professor created only an immediate risk that the other justices would be wary of him until he had proven himself as a colleague in the Court's decision-making environment. For the most part, Scalia has participated effectively within the Court and is reported to be personally well liked by his colleagues. However, for certain cases, Scalia's strident article proved to be a precursor for the tone of his judicial opinions concerning issues in which he disagreed strongly with other justices, both conservatives and liberals.

In the separation of powers cases discussed in Chapter 2 in which Scalia was the lone dissenter, he eschewed diplomacy in explaining his opposition to the majority's views and instead forthrightly condemned his colleagues' reasoning. In *Morrison v. Olson*, concerning the constitutionality of appointing independent counsels to investigate wrongdoing by executive branch officials, Scalia purported to highlight "[t]he utter incompatibility of the Court's approach with our constitutional traditions."[20] He further condemned "the folly of the new system of standardless judicial allocation of powers we adopt today."[21] Scalia concluded his dissenting opinion with an ominous warning about what his colleagues had done to the country: "By its short-sighted action today, I fear the Court has permanently encumbered the Republic with an institution that will do it great harm."[22] Scalia's choice of words—"utter incompatibility," "folly," "standardless," and "short-sighted"—is oriented toward ridicule rather than toward persuasion. By choosing to castigate his colleagues rather than merely express disagreement, Scalia creates risks that the human beings underneath the justices' black judicial robes will take offense and remember the barbs in subsequent cases when they must decide whether or not to agree with Scalia's opinions.

Scalia's *Morrison* dissent is not unique. In many cases, Scalia launches verbal assaults to wound his colleagues and tarnish their judicial reputations rather than to persuade them and the public of the correctness of his views. In *Mistretta v. United States*, the case concerning the constitutionality of the U.S. Sentencing Commission, Scalia declared that the other eight justices' approach to separation of powers jurisprudence "will be disastrous" for the country.[23] Similarly, in a case that recognized a constitutional right for public employees to be free from discrimination due to their political party affiliation, Scalia warned the majority that this decision "may well have disastrous consequences for our political system."[24] Echoing this theme that his colleagues' decisions will be the source of significant harm for the governing system, Scalia hit the other justices even closer to "home" in a case concerning parents' asserted right to ask that their irreparably brain-damaged, comatose child be permitted to die without extraordinary medical intervention. Although the parents did not prevail in this case, all of the justices except Scalia recognized a constitutional right for individuals to decline medical treatment. Scalia ominously warned his colleagues that they would "destroy" the Supreme Court by deciding complex moral issues.[25]

In these and other opinions, Scalia aimed his strident language either explicitly or implicitly at his usual allies as well as his usual opponents. It is probably of little consequence if Scalia harshly criticizes liberal justices with whom he will seldom agree. When he criticizes his fellow conservatives, however, he risks driving a wedge between himself and justices whose votes he will need in future cases that present the possibility of attaining a majority in favor of his preferred position.

More problematic than Scalia's repetitive, shrill warnings about the harm to be caused by his colleagues' decisions are his opinions that employ sarcasm to criticize the views of other justices. For example, early in his career on the Supreme Court, Scalia dissented against a decision that endorsed the use of gender as one consideration in hiring decisions under an affirmative action program to move women into supervisory positions from which they were previously excluded. Scalia, who was a well-known opponent of affirmative action from his writings as a law professor, railed against the decision:

In fact, the only losers in this process are the [white males] of the country, for whom [employment discrimination laws have] been not merely repealed but actually inverted. The irony is that these individuals—predominantly unknown, unaffluent, unorganized—suffer this injustice at the hands of a Court fond of thinking itself the champion of the political impotent.[26]

Because Scalia did not say "a Court that *used to be*" the champion of political minorities, he seemed to imply sarcastically that the Court has never fulfilled its purported role as protector of individuals and groups who are victimized by majoritarian political processes. Such a broad statement appeared calculated to swipe at Warren Court holdovers, Justices Brennan and Marshall, who believed that the Supreme Court had made significant contributions to society in *Brown v. Board of Education* and other subsequent decisions. In addition, the other members of the majority targeted by Scalia's shot, Justices O'Connor, Blackmun, Stevens, and Powell, had all previously supported judicial decisions protecting the rights of women, racial minority groups, or both. They, too, undoubtedly did not share or appreciate Scalia's view about what they had accomplished in previous decisions.

Most striking of all is the personal nature of the attack launched by Scalia's opinion. He did not merely express disagreement with the justices in the majority; he sarcastically accused them of being self-deluded about their role and importance. His use of the word *fondly,* in particular, implied that the justices in the majority were improperly vain or self-aggrandizing in assessing their own performances as Supreme Court justices. In personalizing his attack, Scalia produced an opinion that was profoundly different than most opinions. Most Supreme Court opinions are written to explain justices' reasoning:

The function of an opinion is to persuade people outside the Court—first, the parties to the case, and then others, the legal community and other "court watchers"—that the decision is a reasonable one, reasonably arrived at, with sufficient guidance in the Court's opinion to allow those affected to control "primary conduct."[27]

Scalia's opinion, by contrast, constituted an implicitly personal attack on his colleagues.

In an even more striking example, Scalia sarcastically attacked Justice Thurgood Marshall in a case concerning the risk of discrimination in the selection of jurors for a criminal trial. In writing for the majority, which rejected a white defendant's claim that the exclusion of African-Americans from his jury violated the Sixth Amendment right to have a fair cross section of the community represented on his jury, Scalia blasted Justice Marshall's dissent that raised concerns about racial bias in the criminal justice system. Scalia wrote: "Justice Marshall's dissent rolls out the ultimate weapon, the accusation of insensitivity to racial discrimination—which will lose its intimidating effect if it continues to be fired so randomly."[28] Scalia's sarcasm was evident when he referred to raising issues of racial bias as "rolling out the ultimate weapon." In addition, Scalia's statement that assertions about racial discrimination will "lose [their] intimidating effect" implied that such considerations have deterred justices from making appropriate decisions. Moreover, his claim that "accusation[s]" about racial insensitivity "[continue] to be fired so randomly" implies that liberal justices raise concerns about discrimination too frequently and in inappropriate cases.

Overall, the barb aimed specifically at Marshall has broader, unsettling implications by, in effect, accusing the justices of improperly responding to discrimination claims when, according to Scalia, no such claims exist or the decision should have gone against the alleged discrimination victim. As is often the case in Scalia's attacking opinions, his effort to make his criticism sting his opponents leads him to use broad language that implicitly criticizes many other justices in addition to the specific individuals that he has targeted in the particular opinion.

As discussed in Chapter 2, Scalia is one of the most prolific opinion writers on the Rehnquist Court. Because he chooses to express his views so frequently through concurring and dissenting opinions, there are many occasions each term in which his outspokenness can generate friction with his colleagues on the Court. In 1990, the longtime *New York Times* correspondent at the Supreme Court characterized the previous terms as the "season of snarling justices" because "[o]pinions of the last two years contain some of the most vituperative attacks on other justices in [C]ourt history."[29] Such biting exchanges undoubtedly stemmed from conflicts between liberals and conservatives as a new ideological group gained the upper hand on the Court. Justice Scalia's presence, however, played a major role in this increased conflict because his style and personality led him to make many of the most open and sarcastic attacks on other justices. Such conflicts may affect not only Scalia's influence within the Court but also the Court's image in society.

Attention-grabbing disagreements among the justices can cast doubt on the general belief that the Supreme Court is following established legal principles. Thus, the justices normally take care to use their written opinions to elaborate explanations and rationalizations for their interpretations of the Constitution and challenged statutes. Opinions containing open, personal attacks on fellow justices can harm the Court's image by magnifying perceptions that personal or ideological disputes, rather than legal principles, determine the justices' interpretations of constitutional law. As one observer warned:

[T]here is still a serious cost to public brawling on the bench: The more the justices question each other's basic common sense and good faith, the more they may deplete the reservoir of popular good will that is so essential to their singular role in American life. They might eventually find their rulings dismissed as the work of unelected, unprincipled politicians.[30]

Scalia's Disregard for Precedent

The principle of stare decisis, or adherence to case precedent, has been described as "firmly rooted in [American] jurisprudence."[31] The use of previous judicial decisions as precedents provides stability and predictability in law and reinforces the judicial system's legitimacy by conveying the idea that judges draw from established law rather than make up new answers for each case. Although most justices are willing to change or reverse precedents that they regard as undesirable or wrongly decided, many justices are cautious about discarding precedents for fear of tarnishing the Court's image as a legal institution. In effect, many justices prefer to change constitutional law through gradual and subtle refinements rather than through wholesale, sudden reversals of established precedents.

Most justices feel obligated to pay homage to the importance of precedent, even if they are among those criticized for rewriting case law too suddenly. Chief Justice Rehnquist, for example, has called stare decisis "a cornerstone of our legal system,"[32] even though critics claim that he has eagerly changed case law affecting employment discrimination and prisoners' petitions.[33]

Justice Scalia, by contrast, stands out as a justice who is generally less willing to acknowledge the value of case precedent. Scalia made his views quite clear in cases concerning the admission of victim impact testimony in capital sentencing. Although the Supreme Court had decided against the admission of such testimony in 1987 and 1989,[34] Scalia expressed his disregard for stare decisis with shocking forthrightness that virtually acknowledged the influence of politics and justices' personal viewpoints over the definition of constitutional law. In the 1989 case, Scalia criticized the majority's decision favoring the rights of a criminal defendant and argued for a reversal of the recent precedents by noting that "[o]verrulings of precedent rarely occur without a change in the Court's personnel."[35] Scalia further declared, "I would think it a violation of my oath to adhere to what I consider a plainly unjustified intrusion upon the democratic process in order that the Court might save face."[36] In 1991, after Justice Souter was appointed to the Court, a new majority overruled the prior precedents and permitted victim impact testimony.[37]

By stating his views so bluntly, Scalia deviated from the usual traditions of the Court and disturbed other justices who are concerned about emphasizing stare decisis in order to maintain the Court's image and legitimacy. One of Scalia's concurring opinions that directly attacked a series of precedents concerning juror discretion in death penalty cases led four justices to join an opinion that accused Scalia of threatening "the integrity of this Court's adjudicative process."[38] Retired Justice Lewis Powell issued a veiled criticism of Scalia and his less forthright conservative colleagues who seemed intent on changing existing liberal precedents. According to Powell, sudden efforts to overturn established precedents "represent explicit endorsement of the idea that the Constitution is nothing more than what five justices say it is. This would undermine the rule of law."[39] As a practical matter, the meaning of the Constitution is indeed defined by five or more justices at any given moment in history. Justices are generally loathe to admit that this is true, however, because of the adverse effect on the Supreme Court's image as a legal institution, and thus many justices take the Court's image seriously when deciding specific controversial cases.

Justice Scalia agrees that the Court's image and role as a legal institution are important. However, his view of the Court's role leads him to disregard stare decisis and seek quick reversal of precedents that do not fit with *his* vision of the Court's proper role. Scalia would not agree that the meaning of the Constitution is whatever five justices say it is because he strongly believes that his interpretive theories will lead to the "correct" interpretation of the fundamental document. His clash with other justices over stare decisis stems from his self-righteous confidence that his interpretive approaches are more important than other justices' concerns about the value of case precedent.

Scalia's Interactions with Other Justices

Lawrence Baum has observed that cordial relationships among the justices provide significant benefits for the Court's decision-making capabilities:

Personal relations [among the justices] also can affect the decisional process. A Court in which conflicts are kept under control will be able to maximize consensus in decisions, because members work easily with each other and are relatively willing to compromise. Such a Court also may function more efficiently, because good interpersonal relations speed the process of reaching decisions and resolving internal problems.[40]

Because justices must interact together, frequently for decades, and reach agreement in order to form majority coalitions for specific opinions, the Court has rituals designed to maintain cordial relations, most notably the tradition of each justice shaking hands with every other justice prior to each conference. Despite his likeable personality, Justice Scalia has disrupted the effort to maintain cordial relations because of his firm views and strident opinions. Scalia has also irritated his colleagues with his aggressive behavior during oral arguments.

Each case accepted for oral argument by the Supreme Court is allotted one hour. The attorney for each side has only thirty minutes to present his or her case. Although most attorneys prepare a formal presentation, the justices usually interrupt the attorneys in order to ask questions. If the justices absorb the entire thirty minutes asking questions, the attorney is not given any extra time. Most justices are cognizant of the need to balance the attorney's desire to make a complete presentation and the justices' desire to ask pertinent questions. Justice Scalia, however, has developed a unique reputation for trying to dominate the entire oral argument not only by interrupting the attorneys but also by cutting off his colleagues in midsentence in order to ask his own questions. Justice Powell commented about Scalia's actions during oral argument by saying that "[s]ometimes there's not much time left for the other eight justices to ask questions."[41] In a candid interview, Justice Blackmun described Scalia's behavior:

[Justice Scalia] is and always will be the professor at work. . . . He asks far too many questions, and he takes over the whole argument of the counsel, he will argue with counsel. . . . Even [Justice O'Connor], who asks a lot of questions, a couple of times gets exasperated when [Scalia] interrupts her line of inquiry and goes off on his own. She throws her pencil down and [says,] "umh, umh."[42]

Scalia's penchant for dominating oral argument at the expense of the other justices produced visible irritation on the part of his usual ally Chief Justice Rehnquist. The chief justice keeps track of the attorneys' speaking time, and thus he is keenly aware when specific justices are absorbing time that might be spent exploring additional aspects of a case. In one incident, "[d]uring Scalia's lengthy questioning of an attorney, Rehnquist finally interrupted to tell the attorney, 'You have fifteen minutes remaining. I hope that when you're given the opportunity to do so, you'll address some of your remarks to the question on which the Court voted to grant certiorari.' "[43] Another incident was reported in a national news magazine:

[O]n the job, [Scalia's] abrasive, know-it-all manner often irritates his colleagues. Chief Justice William Rehnquist was so exasperated by Scalia's rudeness during oral argument of a death penalty case last week that he scolded the justice in public. When Scalia interrupted Justice Anthony Kennedy as he questioned an attorney, a scowling Rehnquist leaned over and shook his finger at Scalia while gesturing with his other hand at Kennedy. "It's clear Rehnquist was furious with Scalia," says a lawyer who was there. Oblivious, Scalia continued to talk. Kennedy, bemused, looked on.[44]

David O'Brien, the noted Supreme Court scholar who became personally acquainted with the justices during a year he spent as the administrative assistant to Chief Justice Burger, wrote that "some justices . . . find [Scalia's] outspokenness irritating."[45] The Supreme Court correspondent for the *Los Angeles Times* reported that several justices showed irritation at Scalia's behavior during oral argument:

On a bench lined with solemn gray figures who often sat as silently as pigeons on a railing, Scalia stood out like a talking parrot. . . . Scalia's show did not always play well with the other justices. Several said they wished he would be quiet for a change. On occasion, Byron White would glare down the bench with a look that suggested he would like to put the newest justice into a headlock if it would shut him up. Sandra O'Connor would harrumph slightly when [Scalia] interrupted one of her questions.[46]

Scalia also generated irritation among his colleagues by his desire to argue about cases during the Court's weekly conferences:

Scalia's assertiveness also puts off some of his colleagues. To Rehnquist, Scalia seemed to believe each case had only one possible right answer—his. . . . As chief justice, [Rehnquist] ran an efficient operation. At the conferences, he ensured that each justice got a chance to state an opinion without interruption. . . . Rehnquist cast a frown on anyone who talks too much. The frowns were often directed at Scalia.[47]

It is difficult to know precisely how Scalia's courtroom behavior affects his relationships, interactions, and influence with his colleagues. One of Justice O'Connor's former law clerks told a reporter that it is unlikely that O'Connor is perturbed by Scalia's written attacks directed at her or his irritating behavior during oral argument.[48] Justice Blackmun's description of O'Connor's reaction to Scalia's interruptions seems to indicate otherwise. Moreover, the Supreme Court correspondent for the *Los Angeles Times* reported that Scalia has "trouble containing his irritation with Sandra O'Connor" because, as he has reportedly told his friends, he views her as a "politician" seeking policy compromises rather than as a judge aspiring to create clear rules.[49] As the next chapter will illustrate, because Scalia has aimed specific attacks at O'Connor, his annoyance with her may very well generate reciprocal feelings and reactions.

In any case, Scalia's irritating behavior during oral argument and conference is simply one more manifestation of his self-righteous confidence that his views are correct and that he need not participate fully in the cooperative and strategic interactions that produce compromises and stable majority coalitions on the Supreme Court. Whether or not Scalia's courtroom behavior, in particular, alienates him from his colleagues, as Chapter 4 will discuss in detail, opinions by several justices in important cases provide strong evidence that Scalia's strident opinions and individualistic views have diminished the potential for decision-making cohesiveness among the Court's conservatives.

NOTES

1. William H. Rehnquist, *The Supreme Court: How It Was, How It Is* (New York: William Morrow, 1987), p. 291.

2. Minersville v. Gobitis, 310 U.S. 586 (1940).

3. West Virginia State Board of Education v. Barnette, 319 U.S. 624 (1943).

4. See H. W. Perry, Jr., *Deciding to Decide* (Cambridge, Mass.: Harvard University Press, 1991).

5. Walter F. Murphy, *Elements of Judicial Strategy* (Chicago: University of Chicago Press, 1964).

6. David J. Danelski, "The Influence of the Chief Justice in the Decisional Process of the Supreme Court," in *American Court Systems*, 2nd ed., eds. Sheldon Goldman and Austin Sarat (New York: Longman, 1989), pp. 486–499.

7. See James F. Simon, *The Antagonists: Hugo Black, Felix Frankfurter, and Civil Liberties in Modern America* (New York: Simon & Schuster, 1989).

8. See J. Woodford Howard, "On Fluidity of Judicial Choice," *American Political Science Review* 62 (1968): 48–49.

9. David Kaplan, "A Master Builder," *Newsweek*, 30 July 1990, pp. 19–20.

10. Christopher E. Smith, "The Supreme Court in Transition: Assessing the Legitimacy of the Leading Legal Institution," *Kentucky Law Journal* 79 (1990–91): 320–321.

11. Enmund v. Florida, 458 U.S. 782 (1982).

12. Ibid., p. 801.

13. Tison v. Arizona, 481 U.S. 137 (1987).

14. Ibid., p. 137.

15. Lawrence Baum, *The Supreme Court*, 3rd ed. (Washington, D.C.: Congressional Quarterly Press, 1989), p. 149.

16. Regents of the University of California v. Bakke, 438 U.S. 265 (1978).

17. Antonin Scalia, "The Disease as Cure," *Washington University Law Quarterly* (1979): 147–148.

18. Ibid., pp. 152–153.

19. Ibid., p. 153.

20. Morrison v. Olson, 103 S. Ct. 2597, 2628 (1988) (Scalia, J., dissenting).

21. Ibid., p. 2631.

22. Ibid., p. 2640.

23. Mistretta v. United States, 109 S. Ct. 647, 683 (Scalia, J., dissenting).

24. Rutan v. Republican Party of Illinois, 110 S. Ct. 2729 (1990) (Scalia, J., dissenting).

25. Cruzan v. Missouri, 110 S. Ct. 2841, 2863 (1990) (Scalia, J., concurring).

26. Johnson v. Transportation Agency, Santa Clara County, 107 S. Ct. 1442, 1476 (1987) (Scalia, J., dissenting).

27. Stephen Wasby, *The Supreme Court in the Federal Judicial System* (Chicago: Nelson-Hall, 1988), p. 263.

28. Holland v. Illinois, 110 S. Ct. 803, 810 (1990).

29. Stuart Taylor, "Season of Snarling Justices," *Akron Beacon Journal*, 5 April 1990, p. A11.

30. Ibid.

31. Harold Grilliot and Frank Schubert, *Introduction to Law and the Legal System*, 4th ed. (Boston: Houghton Mifflin, 1989), p. 164.

32. Webster v. Reproductive Health Services, 109 S. Ct. 3040, 3056 (1989).

33. Robert Glennon, "Will the Real Conservatives Please Stand Up?" *American Bar Association Journal*, 76 (1 August 1990): 50.

34. Booth v. Maryland, 482 U.S. 496 (1987); South Carolina v. Gathers, 109 S. Ct. 2207 (1989).

35. South Carolina v. Gathers, 109 S. Ct. 2207, 2217 (1989) (Scalia, J., dissenting).

36. Ibid., p. 2218.

37. Payne v. Tennessee, 111 S. Ct. 2597 (1991).

38. Walton v. Arizona 110 S. Ct. 3047 (1990), discussed in Linda Greenhouse, "Supreme Court Dissenters: Loners or Pioneers?" *New York Times*, 20 July 1990, p. B7.

39. Glennon, p. 51.

40. Baum, p. 156.

41. David Kaplan and Bob Cohn, "The Court's Mr. Right," *Newsweek*, 5 November 1990, p. 67.

42. Stuart Taylor, "Blackmun Provides a Peek at the People under Those Robes," *New York Times*, 25 July 1988, p. B6.

43. David O'Brien, *Storm Center: The Supreme Court in American Politics*, 2nd ed. (New York: W. W. Norton, 1990), p. 274.

44. "Rude Robes," *Newsweek*, 19 October 1992, p. 5.

45. O'Brien, p. 274.

46. David G. Savage, *Turning Right: The Making of the Rehnquist Court* (New York: John Wiley & Sons, 1992), p. 119.

47. Ibid., p. 201.

48. Linda Greenhouse, "Name-calling in the Supreme Court: When the Justices Vent Their Spleen, Is There a Social Cost?" *New York Times*, 28 July 1989, p. B10.

49. Savage, p. 202.

Justice Scalia and the Failure of the Conservative Agenda

Justice Scalia's independent viewpoints and outspokenness adversely affected the efforts by political conservatives to use the Supreme Court to advance key policy interests and thereby reverse liberal judicial policies from the Warren and Burger Court eras. Despite the success of Presidents Reagan and Bush in appointing enough conservative justices to the Supreme Court to form a dominant majority, the new majority did not act during its moment of opportunity to eliminate key precedents that were objectionable to conservatives. After his appointment to the Supreme Court, Scalia was viewed by "adoring conservatives . . . [as] the savior who will lead them into the judicial promised land of 'strict construction.' "[1] Scalia was willing to use his intellect and skills to advance his conservative judicial philosophy, but aspects of his philosophy and judicial behavior made him ill-suited to the task of leading the Supreme Court's emerging conservative majority.

SCALIA'S THEMES AND LIBERAL OUTCOMES

As described in Chapter 2, Scalia's interpretive themes, including textualism, originalism, and efforts to reduce judicial intervention into cases, guide his decision-making behavior. In most instances, Scalia's interpretive approach leads him to join his conservative colleagues because he views liberal justices as too willing to interpret the Constitution's words flexibly in order to expand civil rights and liberties at the expense of governmental power. In other cases, however, Scalia's textualist approach leads him to join the Court's liberals when he believes that the words of the Bill of Rights mandate a result that protects the rights of individuals.

Other conservative justices frequently focus on the policy consequences of civil liberties issues in order to advance their preferred outcomes. For example, in creating a "good faith" exception to the exclusionary rule, Justice White used the language of "cost/benefit analysis" to justify his conservative policy choice to limit restraints on police officers during warrantless searches: "[We] conclude that the marginal or nonexistent benefits produced by suppressing evidence obtained in objectively reasonable reliance on a subsequently invalidated search warrant cannot justify the substantial costs to society of exclusion."[2] By contrast, Scalia surprised many people—and disappointed many of his conservative admirers—when he joined the Court's liberals in two highly controversial cases that decided the burning of the American flag during political protests is constitutionally protected freedom of expression.[3] Because of his emphasis on the text of the Constitution, Scalia apparently believed that the forthrightly stated protection of freedom of speech in the First Amendment prevented prosecution of even an offensive form of political expression.

Scalia's strongly held, independent viewpoints have made him an obstacle to the conservatives' attainment of several policy objectives, especially some in the area of criminal defendants' rights.

The Exclusionary Rule

The "exclusionary rule" is one of the most controversial and harshly criticized policy products of the Warren Court era. Under the exclusionary rule, if law enforcement officers obtain evidence improperly, it may not be used against criminal defendants. The Supreme Court enunciated the rule as a means to protect citizens' Fourth Amendment rights against unreasonable searches and seizures. Political conservatives have long criticized the exclusionary rule because it can permit guilty criminal defendants to go free if the police fail to follow proper procedures. The exclusionary rule was first applied by the Supreme Court in 1914, but its initial application only affected actions by federal law enforcement officers (i.e., the FBI, U.S. marshals, etc.).[4] Because most crimes are governed by state laws and enforced by local police, the Supreme Court's exclusionary rule initially had no impact on most of the law enforcement activities undertaken throughout the country.

During the twentieth century, the Supreme Court gradually began to apply individual provisions of the Bill of Rights to protect citizens against actions by state and local governments as well as by those of the federal government. The Court's initial interpretation of the Bill of Rights in 1833 declared that the Constitution provides people with rights only against the federal government and not against state and local officials.[5] In 1925, the Supreme Court declared that the First Amendment's protection of freedom of speech protected people against state and local governments, too.[6] Shortly thereafter, the Court also applied freedom of the press against state and local governments.[7] In the years that followed, claimants presented the Supreme Court with other provisions of the Bill of Rights in hopes that the justices would give people additional constitutional protections against state and local government interference. Until the 1950s, the justices were generally reluctant to expand too rapidly the scope of protections for individuals.

In 1949, the Supreme Court was asked to apply the Fourth Amendment's exclusionary rule against the states, but the majority declined to do so.[8] In an opinion by Justice Felix Frankfurter, the Court acknowledged that people should be protected against unreasonable searches and seizures by state and local officials, but the justices said that the exclusionary rule was not necessary to ensure compliance by local law enforcement officials. According to Justice Frankfurter, states and localities should develop their own remedies for unlawful searches, such as disciplining police officers for misconduct or permitting civil suits against the police department. Frankfurter also expressed his belief that public opinion in a local community would deter improper searches by police, and therefore he deemed the exclusionary rule to be necessary only against federal officials. In 1952, Frankfurter applied an ad hoc exclusionary rule against local police for entering a home without a warrant and forcibly extracting pills from a man's stomach, first by pummeling the man and later by forcing him to vomit at the hospital.[9] However, Frankfurter and the other justices applied the exclusionary rule only to situations that "shocked the conscience," and thus the rule did not apply to all situations in which police officers violated people's Fourth Amendment rights.

By the 1960s, the composition of the Court had changed. Earl Warren had become chief justice, and his ally, William Brennan, had been appointed by President Dwight D. Eisenhower to join such liberal Roosevelt-appointee holdovers as William O. Douglas and Hugo Black. Gradually, the Court began to apply more provisions of the Bill of Rights to state and local governments. In 1961, in the famous case of *Mapp v. Ohio*, a six-member majority applied the exclusionary rule across the board to all civilian law enforcement officers.[10] In his opinion for the Court, Justice Tom Clark explained that the exclusionary rule was needed to prevent unlawful searches because other remedies, as proposed by Frankfurter in 1949, had proven to be ineffective. Police officers across the country complained that the Warren Court was favoring the rights of criminals over the interests of society, although subsequent social science studies showed that exclusionary rule issues actually affected relatively few cases.[11] Political conservatives regarded the *Mapp* decision as an improper judicial interference with the local administration of justice, and President Richard Nixon's first "law and order" appointee, Chief Justice Warren Burger, issued a stinging critique of the exclusionary rule in a 1971 dissenting opinion.[12]

During the Burger Court era, the Nixon appointees, joined by Justice White, managed to narrow the application of the exclusionary rule by creating various exceptions. In a series of cases in 1984, the Court declared that improperly obtained evidence could still be used to prosecute defendants in a variety of specific circumstances: (1) if it would have been inevitably discovered eventually during a lawful search;[13] (2) if the police in "good faith" reasonably believed that their improper search was actually proper;[14] or (3) if the impropriety (e.g., improper questioning of arrestee) occurred while the police attempted to protect the immediate safety of the public.[15] Other case decisions created additional refinements in the exclusionary rule without abolishing it.

The Preservation of a Controversial Rule

When Justice Scalia was appointed to the Court in 1986, President Ronald Reagan's attorney general had been issuing highly publicized condemnations of Warren Court–era decisions protecting the rights of criminal defendants.[16] Presumably, the Reagan administration expected that Scalia, a well-known conservative, shared its views on the Warren Court's liberal judicial policies. Only two justices who consistently supported the exclusionary rule, the Warren-era holdovers Brennan and Marshall, remained on the Supreme Court. The other justices were either consistent critics of the rule or supporters of the rule only in some circumstances; so there existed an opportunity for a new conservative to provide a decisive vote to curtail significantly, if not abolish, the judicial policy that had long been objectionable to conservative politicians. In his very first term on the Court, Scalia indicated that he did not share the other conservatives' determination to eliminate the exclusionary rule policy. Scalia's interpretive themes, as described in Chapter 2, took precedence over the policy outcome preferred by his conservative colleagues.

In *Arizona v. Hicks*, police properly entered an apartment without a warrant to investigate someone who fired shots from an upstairs apartment through the floor into a downstairs apartment.[17] In addition to finding weapons in the apartment, police also noticed two sets of expensive stereo equipment that seemed out of place in the "squalid and otherwise ill-appointed four-room apartment."[18] The officers moved some of the stereo components in order to locate the serial numbers and reported the numbers by telephone to the police station. The officers were informed that the stereo equipment had been stolen during a robbery. The defendant sought to have the stereo equipment excluded as evidence because the officers had violated the "plain view" doctrine established in *Coolidge v. New Hampshire*.[19] The *Coolidge* doctrine limits warrantless searches to items within plain view during lawful searches of private areas.

Justice Scalia joined the most liberal justices (Brennan, Marshall, Blackmun, and Stevens; White concurred separately in the result) and wrote the majority opinion supporting the claim of the criminal defendant that the evidence ought to be excluded because of an improper search. In dissent, Chief Justice Rehnquist and Justices O'Connor and Powell sought to reduce the restraint imposed on the police in such circumstances. The conservative dissenters would have required the police to have only "reasonable suspicions" rather than "probable cause" to believe that the items were stolen before undertaking a warrantless search of the property.[20]

Scalia, however, took a strong opposing stand by declaring that the police officers' actions in moving the stereo equipment to locate the serial numbers constituted a search under the Fourth Amendment that required them to have "probable cause." According to Scalia, "taking action, unrelated to the objectives of the authorized intrusion . . . produce[d] a new invasion of [the defendant's] privacy unjustified by the exigent circumstances that validated the entry."21 In other words, although the police could enter the apartment without a warrant to investigate immediately a reported shooting and to look for weapons, they could only look at those portions of other items that were in plain view; they could not pick up the stereo equipment or other items that were not related to the shooting.

Unlike the three conservative justices in dissent, Scalia was not looking for a way to modify the exclusionary rule in order to justify police actions that, on the surface, may have appeared to be trivial. How harmful is it, after all, for the police to move stereo equipment in order to read the serial numbers on the back or bottom? From Scalia's perspective, however, with his clear-sighted view that the provisions of the Constitution have definite and specific meanings based on their words and their original meanings, the Fourth Amendment precluded such actions—even if it meant excluding probative evidence that could be used to convict a guilty defendant of robbery and possessing stolen property.

Scalia's decision to join the liberals in support of the rights of a guilty criminal defendant rather than to advocate modification of the exclusionary rule was also consistent with his theme of keeping cases out of the federal courts and limiting judicial involvement in cases. Scalia turned aside assertions by the state of Arizona that the evidence should have been admitted under an expanded good faith exception to the exclusionary rule because, according to Arizona, the officers did not knowingly do anything wrong in moving the stereo equipment. In keeping with his desire to limit the scope of the Supreme Court's decision making, Scalia simply declared that the good faith exception "was not the question on which certiorari was granted, and we decline to consider it."22

The Supreme Court sometimes decides cases on grounds other than the issue that was presented to the justices. For example, the landmark exclusionary rule case, *Mapp v. Ohio*, was presented to the justices as a First Amendment case because the defendant was arrested after police found pornographic materials during a warrantless search. The justices, however, used the case as a vehicle to establish an important Fourth Amendment precedent about search and seizure.[23] By contrast, in *Arizona v. Hicks*, Scalia declined the opportunity to expand the good faith exception to the exclusionary rule even though he made his support for the exception clear in two other cases decided during the same term.[24] His inclination to avoid overreaching by the Court in order to achieve justices' policy preferences apparently led him to disagree with other conservative justices who sought to justify the police officers' actions and further weaken the exclusionary rule.

Scalia's decision in *Arizona v. Hicks* is also understandable in terms of his thematic preference for reducing litigants' access to the federal courts. The plain view doctrine under *Coolidge* was a "bright-line" rule that all police officers could understand because the rule was simple and clear and had no exceptions to complicate their understanding. From the perspective of Scalia's preference for limiting cases in the federal courts, a bright-line rule that does not unduly burden law enforcement officers could limit appeals without freeing culpable offenders.

A change in the plain view doctrine, however, would invite many new cases to test the newly developing boundaries of the blurred rule. If police officers were permitted to deviate from the plain view doctrine by moving a stereo six inches in order to look at the serial numbers, there would probably be a flood of subsequent cases asking the Court to decide whether police can move objects eight inches, twelve inches, turn them upside down, remove a front cover, or otherwise move beyond simply looking at things that are in plain view. Maintenance of the exclusionary rule by keeping the plain view doctrine in place permitted one defendant, Hicks, from having evidence used against him, but it also prevented the potential problems that would come from inviting additional litigants to test the boundaries of a new rule.[25]

Scalia joined the conservatives in nearly all criminal justice cases during his first term,[26] and during his first six terms (1986–92), he was second only to Rehnquist in his disinclination to support claims by criminal defendants and prisoners. Rehnquist supported conservative outcomes in 91 percent of nonunanimous criminal justice cases, and Scalia supported conservative outcomes in 86 percent of such cases.[27] As indicated by *Arizona v. Hicks*, however, Scalia's interpretive philosophy and jurisprudential priorities led him to disagree with other conservative justices in certain categories of cases, especially concerning the Confrontation Clause and search and seizure. Conservative politicians had hoped that the Rehnquist Court would seize opportunities to reshape judicial policy decisions in favor of law enforcement officials' discretionary actions, but Scalia declined to pursue such policy-oriented motivations when those motivations clashed with his unique interpretive themes and priorities.

STRIDENCY, ALIENATION, AND THE PRESERVATION OF ABORTION

Because antiabortion interest groups were such a powerful, vocal, and well-organized constituency within the Republican party, Presidents Reagan and Bush both hoped that their nominees to the Supreme Court would reverse *Roe v. Wade,*[28] the controversial Burger Court–era decision that established a woman's right of choice concerning abortion as an element of the constitutional right to privacy. Reagan and Bush succeeded in appointing justices who disagreed with the members of the majority in *Roe* and who favored permitting states to place greater restrictions on the availability of abortion. However, the new appointees failed by one vote to achieve political conservatives' primary objective of erasing *Roe*. Justice Scalia played a key role in the abortion controversy because he was the Court's most vocal opponent of *Roe*.

Unlike the exclusionary rule example in which Scalia's interpretive themes hindered the success of the conservatives' policy objectives, Scalia contributed to the preservation of *Roe* because of the stridency of his opinions concerning abortion. Scalia's opinions helped to defeat his own objective because his opinions attacked both allies and opponents for failing to agree with the correctness of his strong views.

After the mid-nineteenth century, state legislatures throughout the United States made it a crime to perform abortions. In the 1960s, however, several states began to liberalize their laws to permit abortions when a doctor determined that a woman's health would be endangered by a full-term pregnancy. A few states, including Hawaii,[29] became magnets for women seeking abortions either because the previous restrictive laws had been set aside or because some doctors within those states freely determined that nearly any pregnant woman seeking an abortion qualified under the exception for protecting women's health.

Throughout this period, Texas had especially strict criminal laws against doctors performing abortions. In 1970, a poor woman who claimed that she became pregnant after being raped found two young lawyers willing to challenge the Texas statute as violative of the woman's constitutional rights. The Texas statute prevented her from obtaining the abortion that she sought, yet she was too poor to afford to travel to other states where abortions were more easily available.

When the case reached the Supreme Court in 1973, the Burger Court generated decades of political conflict by invalidating all state laws prohibiting abortion. In the landmark case of *Roe v. Wade*,[30] the Court supported the woman's challenge against the Texas statute that made it a criminal offense to obtain or attempt an abortion unless the mother's life was endangered by the pregnancy. Justice Harry Blackmun's opinion for the Court identified a right of choice for abortion during the first six months of pregnancy as a component of the constitutional right to privacy. During the second trimester of pregnancy (months four through six), states were permitted to regulate how abortions would be performed in order to protect the health of women, but states could not bar abortions prior to the seventh month of pregnancy when the fetus was regarded as "viable," meaning capable of living outside the mother's womb.

Although the *Roe* decision was controversial, a solid seven-member majority on the Court supported abortion as a protected right under the Constitution. The justices in the majority included Warren Court liberals, Justices William Brennan, Thurgood Marshall, and William O. Douglas; a Warren-era moderate, Justice Potter Stewart; and three of Nixon's Republican appointees, Justices Lewis Powell and Harry Blackmun and Chief Justice Warren Burger. The only dissenters were Kennedy appointee Justice Byron White and Nixon appointee Justice William Rehnquist.

The *Roe* decision was highly controversial not only because it endorsed a policy that many Americans opposed but also because Blackmun's opinion applied a flexible approach to constitutional interpretation in order to reach the result favoring a right of choice. The right to privacy is not mentioned in the Bill of Rights. It was established through flexible interpretation of the Constitution by the Warren Court liberals in the 1960s.[31] The *Roe* opinion took the right to privacy, which itself was a matter of dispute among legal scholars and judges, and declared that choices about abortion are a component of this controversial right. Many conservatives believe that the Court's opinions on privacy and abortion are the quintessential examples of liberal judicial activism in which the meaning of the Constitution is expanded to endorse policy concepts that are not reflected in either the words or the original meaning of the document.

In the years following the *Roe* decision, the Supreme Court found itself faced with the abortion issue in various forms again and again. The Court's decision in *Roe v. Wade* defined national abortion policy in a manner that clashed with the views of a large minority of the American population. Many religious denominations, most notably the Catholic church, believe that abortion is impermissible because it entails ending a human life. Because this minority believed strongly that the Supreme Court's policy decision was wrong, antiabortion interest groups mobilized to undertake political activities in opposition to a right of choice for abortion.[32] Antiabortion interest groups sponsored public relations campaigns, protest marches, and lobbying efforts aimed at persuading elected officials and the general public to oppose the pro-choice policy established by the Supreme Court's decision.

The antiabortion groups succeeded in persuading Congress and some state legislatures to challenge the judicial policy announced in *Roe v. Wade*. Members of Congress reacted to the decision in *Roe v. Wade* by threatening a variety of legislative proposals aimed at changing the abortion policy announced by the Supreme Court. The legislative efforts to initiate a constitutional amendment to ban abortion and to limit judicial jurisdiction over abortion issues never gained sufficient support within the legislature for enactment.[33] Congress did succeed, however, in passing legislation that barred federal government funding for abortions sought by poor women.

When the restriction on public funding for abortions was challenged in the judicial system, a deeply divided Supreme Court endorsed the congressional action as permissible under the Constitution.[34] The majority asserted that the loss of funding did not deprive anyone of their right to choose to have an abortion. Poor women were merely deprived of the means to obtain abortions. The Court also declared that the U.S. Constitution permitted state legislatures to impose similar limitations upon the use of state funds for poor women's abortions.[35]

The Akron Case

State and local legislative bodies attempted to make even more significant and direct challenges to the Supreme

Court's decision in *Roe*. The city of Akron, Ohio, for example, passed a municipal ordinance that purported to comply with *Roe*'s provision for reasonable regulations designed to protect the health of the mother during the second trimester of pregnancy. The ordinance sought to impose several restrictions on abortions within the city:

(1) [A]ll abortions performed after the first trimester had to be performed in a hospital, (2) abortions were prohibited for unmarried minors under age 15 without parental consent or court order, (3) the physician had to inform the woman of various facts concerning the operation, (4) abortions were delayed for at least twenty-four hours after the woman's consent, and (5) the physician had to insure that fetal remains were disposed of in a "humane and sanitary manner."[36]

On the surface, Akron's restrictions appeared to be reasonable, but the underlying details within the city's restrictions included direct challenges to the Supreme Court's decision in *Roe*. Most notably, the ordinance required doctors to inform women that "the unborn child is a human life from the moment of conception."[37] This provision clashed directly with the Court's opinion in *Roe*. The Supreme Court had expressly stated in *Roe* that the beginning of human life could not be precisely defined: "When those trained in the respective disciplines of medicine, philosophy, and theology are unable to arrive at a consensus, the judiciary, at this point in the development of man's knowledge, is not in a position to speculate as to the [beginning point of life]."[38] The Burger Court majority had little patience with thinly disguised attacks on its policy decision, and it struck down the entire Akron ordinance as well as other state and local laws that attempted to regulate abortion and thereby hinder women's choices.[39]

Although a majority of justices continued to strike down statutes limiting abortion until 1989, the 1983 Akron case marked the beginning of a pivotal turning point because it

was the first case in which a Reagan appointee participated
in the Court's abortion decisions. In 1981, Reagan appointed
Sandra Day O'Connor to replace retiring Justice Potter Stewart, a member of the original *Roe* majority. Most of the nation
applauded the fulfillment of President Reagan's pledge to
appoint the first woman to the Supreme Court, but antiabortion groups opposed O'Connor's nomination. The opposition stemmed from actions taken by O'Connor as a member
of the Arizona state senate in which she voted on some bills
that affected abortion without vigorously opposing abortion
in all circumstances. To most observers, however, O'Connor's
views on abortion were uncertain, and she came to the Supreme Court with a reputation as a loyal Republican and a
conservative state appellate judge.

In the Akron case, O'Connor joined Chief Justice Rehnquist and Justice White, the original *Roe* dissenters, in opposing the majority's decision to strike down the city ordinance.
O'Connor pleased both President Reagan and her former
opponents among the antiabortion groups by authoring a
dissenting opinion that presented a strong critique of Justice
Blackmun's reasoning in *Roe*. In a general comment within
the opinion, O'Connor's words embodied the essence of the
political conservatives' criticisms of *Roe v. Wade* and the other
objectionable precedents from the Warren and Burger Court
eras:

Irrespective of what we may believe is wise or prudent policy in
this difficult area, "the Constitution does not constitute us as
'Platonic Guardians' nor does it vest in this Court the authority to
strike down laws because they do not meet our standards of
desirable social policy, 'wisdom,' or 'common sense.' "[40]

In her specific discussion of abortion, O'Connor criticized
Blackmun's trimester framework in *Roe* as "a completely
unworkable method of accommodating the conflicting personal rights and compelling state interests that are involved
in the abortion context."[41] O'Connor objected to linking

constitutional interpretation with any current state of medical technology by noting that advances in technology may change the point of viability and thereby completely undercut Blackmun's premise that the end of the second trimester marks the point of viability when states can prohibit abortion.

O'Connor's opinion demonstrated that support for *Roe* among the justices had diminished, and only six justices continued to support the landmark precedent in 1983. The appointment of Justice Scalia in 1986 brought to the Court a strident opponent of the judicial abortion policy who had criticized *Roe* in a law review article prior to becoming a judge.[42] When Justice Powell, a member of the original *Roe* majority and author of the Court's pro-choice opinion in the Akron case, retired in 1987, the political conservatives appeared to have their opportunity to gain the fifth vote necessary to overturn *Roe v. Wade*. Because President Reagan's first nominee to replace Powell, Judge Robert Bork, was known to oppose the Court's reasoning that established the right to privacy and the right of choice for abortion, pro-choice interest groups joined a variety of liberal civil rights groups in successfully fighting against his confirmation. Powell's eventual replacement, federal appellate judge Anthony Kennedy, was known as a conservative Republican judge, but his views on abortion were not known. Through a quirk of history, the two dissenters from *Roe*, Rehnquist and White, remained on the Court, while members of the *Roe* majority gradually retired and were replaced by more conservative justices.

The Missouri Case

The conservative justices' opportunity to change abortion policy arrived in 1989 in a case challenging a Missouri statute that prohibited the performance of abortions at public hospitals, required doctors to conduct viability tests before performing abortions, and proclaimed that human life begins at conception. In a monumental five-to-four decision (*Webster v. Reproductive Health Services*), the three Reagan appointees joined the holdover *Roe* dissenters, Rehnquist and White, to uphold the state law and thereby invite legislatures for the first time to begin enacting legislation intended to limit the availability of abortion.[43]

In the majority opinion, Chief Justice Rehnquist endorsed all aspects of the Missouri law, including the preamble that declared "[t]he life of each human being begins at conception" and "unborn children have protectable interests in life, health, and well being."[44] These statements directly contradicted Blackmun's admonition in *Roe* that states should not attempt to define when life begins. Moreover, the Rehnquist Court's acceptance of this portion of the statute contradicted the Burger Court's rejection of such language in the Akron case. Rehnquist and the other justices in the majority claimed that the preamble could stand because it had no substantive legal effect. Because the Court's composition had changed, the conservatives were in a position to dismantle *Roe*. However, although they were positioned to dismantle *Roe*, they did not actually fulfill the ultimate hopes of antiabortion groups and President Reagan.

The five-member majority weakened *Roe* by approving new kinds of state regulations, but it did not overturn *Roe* because Justice O'Connor indicated that she was not prepared to reexamine *Roe* in considering the Missouri statute at issue in *Webster*. O'Connor argued that the Missouri statute did not "conflict with any of the Court's past decisions concerning state regulation of abortion. Therefore, there is no necessity to reexamine the constitutional validity of *Roe v. Wade*."[45] O'Connor's decision not to overturn *Roe* in this case did not constitute an endorsement of the controversial precedent. O'Connor merely indicated that a reexamination of *Roe* should be deferred until there was a case that directly challenged her understanding of *Roe*. O'Connor gave hope to anti-abortion forces about her future actions by referring to her dissent in the Akron case and commenting on *"Roe*'s trimester framework which I continue to consider problematic."[46]

Because Justice O'Connor was not yet willing to provide the fifth vote necessary for reversal of *Roe*, Chief Justice Rehnquist, joined by Justices White and Kennedy, claimed to agree that "[t]his case affords us no occasion to revisit the holding of *Roe*," which, unlike this case concerning a Missouri regulatory statute, concerned a Texas statute that criminalized abortions.[47] Thus, Rehnquist, White, and Kennedy admitted that they were "modify[ing] and narrow[ing] *Roe*" but leaving the landmark precedent in place.[48] Rehnquist, White, and Kennedy would not take the risk of advocating outright reversal of *Roe* until they were sure of O'Connor's support for fear that asserting too strong a position against abortion might push O'Connor to join the liberals in setting yet another precedent endorsing *Roe*. Rehnquist and his allies claimed to agree with O'Connor's assertion that *Roe* did not need to be reexamined in this case, yet they also sought to persuade O'Connor of *Roe*'s fatal flaws by detailing their reasons why the *Roe* opinion was inconsistent with the Constitution:

[T]he rigid *Roe* framework is hardly consistent with the notion of a Constitution cast in general terms, as ours is, and usually speaking in general principles, as ours does. The key elements of the *Roe* framework—trimesters and viability—are not found in the text of the Constitution or in any place else one would expect to find a constitutional principle. Since the bounds of the inquiry are essentially indeterminate, the result has been a web of legal rules that have become increasingly intricate, resembling a code or regulation rather than a body of constitutional doctrine.[49]

In their strategic action of seeking to persuade O'Connor while indicating a willingness to wait for her to make a decision, Rehnquist, White, and Kennedy sought to cultivate her support for any subsequent case that would challenge *Roe* more directly.

While Rehnquist, with the support of White and Kennedy, strategically crafted his opinion to express opposition to *Roe* while endeavoring to gain O'Connor's support in the future, Scalia employed his characteristic stridency to attack his conservative allies, especially O'Connor, for being unwilling to wipe away the *Roe* precedent once and for all. In his concurring opinion, Scalia used all of his strongest techniques, including sarcasm, personal attacks, and dire warnings of impending catastrophe, to condemn his colleagues. Scalia sarcastically derided Rehnquist's majority opinion:

The outcome of today's case will undoubtedly be heralded as a triumph of judicial statesmanship. It is not that, unless it is statesmanlike needlessly to prolong this Court's self-awarded sovereignty over a field where it has little proper business since the answers to most of the cruel questions posed are political and not juridical.[50]

Scalia directed a special attack at O'Connor for failing to come out against *Roe*. In a strong statement, Scalia declared that "Justice O'Connor's assertion that a 'fundamental rule of judicial restraint' requires us to avoid reconsidering *Roe, cannot be taken seriously*" [emphasis supplied].[51] Supreme Court justices are accustomed to disagreeing strongly with each other's reasoning. However, words that imply such a complete and belittling rejection of a colleague's opinion are out of step with the usual strategic diplomacy employed by justices to cultivate support from each other. Scalia proceeded to devote fully half of his opinion to attacking O'Connor for authoring and joining opinions in other comparable situations that reexamined precedents despite not facing direct challenges to those precedents. The opinion made it very clear that one of Scalia's primary purposes was to implicitly label O'Connor as a "hypocrite" for refusing to tackle the abortion issue in circumstances in which she had previously addressed directly a variety of other controversial issues.

In addition to his lengthy personal attack on O'Connor, Scalia issued ominous warnings to all of his conservative colleagues that their failure to overturn *Roe* immediately did "great damage [to] the Court [by] mak[ing] it the object of the sort of organized public pressure that political institutions in a democracy ought to receive."[52] Scalia further asserted that the other justices were "continuously distort[ing] the public perception of the role of this Court."[53] He concluded his opinion by accusing his conservative colleagues of taking "the least responsible" course of action by avoiding a direct reexamination and reversal of *Roe*.[54]

Scalia's concurring opinion was a quintessential example of his failure to adhere to the Court's usual traditions of diplomatic opinions and strategic interactions in order to cultivate the support of colleagues. While Rehnquist and the other conservatives were building a bridge between themselves and O'Connor by laying the groundwork for O'Connor to join their open opposition to *Roe* in a future case, Scalia was tossing gasoline on the bridge and igniting it. Could O'Connor be expected to provide the crucial fifth vote in a subsequent case when she had endured such a strident and personal attack? O'Connor might have felt that she risked the appearance of being pounded into submission if she were to agree with Scalia in a later case. Indeed, after such a strident attack, nearly any human being in an authoritative position would feel more inclined to defend him- or herself rather than give the appearance of acquiescence. One can only imagine what Chief Justice Rehnquist and Justices White and Kennedy thought as they read Scalia's "slash and burn" concurring opinion after they carefully crafted a majority opinion that sought to agree with O'Connor and persuade her to join them in a future case.

The Lost Opportunity in 1992: The Pennsylvania Case

The Supreme Court's next opportunity to overturn *Roe v. Wade* came in 1992 in a challenge to a Pennsylvania statute that regulated abortions through various provisions requiring such things as a waiting period, parental consent for minor girls, and notification of husbands. By this time, two more members of the original *Roe* majority, Justices Brennan and Marshall, had retired and been replaced by Bush appointees, Justices Souter and Thomas. It appeared that only one vote was needed from either O'Connor, Souter, or Thomas to give the outspoken members of the *Webster* majority—Rehnquist, Scalia, White, and Kennedy—the support they needed to overturn *Roe*.

Justice Thomas, despite having claimed during his confirmation hearings that he had never discussed the issue of abortion with anyone in the nearly two decades since *Roe* was decided, jumped immediately into the conservative camp. His vote was consistent with his general pattern of joining the Court's most conservative justices, Rehnquist and Scalia, in more than 75 percent of cases during his freshman term.[55] However, Thomas did not provide the needed fifth vote to achieve political conservatives' dream of overturning *Roe*. Justice Kennedy defeated the reversal by surprisingly deserting his conservative colleagues in order to join Souter and O'Connor in coauthoring a majority opinion (*Planned Parenthood v. Casey*) that approved most of the regulations but also explicitly reaffirmed *Roe*.[56]

Justices O'Connor, Souter, and Kennedy coauthored an unusual joint majority opinion that emphasized the need to protect the Supreme Court's image and legitimacy by providing stability in law. Because *Roe v. Wade* had been the law of the land for nearly two decades and had been relied upon by millions of women, the three justices indicated that they did not wish to change the law overnight simply because the composition of the Court had changed. According to the three justices:

The Court must take care to speak and act in ways that allow people to accept its decisions on the terms the Court claims for them, as grounded truly in principle, not as compromises with social and political pressures having, as such, no bearing on the principled choices that the Court is obliged to make.[57]

Thus, O'Connor, Souter, and Kennedy defended *Roe* for the sake of reinforcing the importance of case precedent by declaring that a decision to overrule *Roe* would be "at the cost of both profound and unnecessary damage to the Court's legitimacy, and to the Nation's commitment to the rule of law."[58]

Because the Court's decision came only a few months before the Republicans lost control of the White House in the 1992 elections, the surprisingly strong reaffirmation of *Roe* appeared to preclude any possibility that political conservatives would achieve a primary policy objective that had motivated the selection of conservative justices for the Supreme Court during the 1980s and early 1990s. When the justices finally confronted the issue of reversing *Roe* directly, two Reagan appointees (O'Connor and Kennedy) and one Bush appointee (Souter) disappointed their conservative backers and authored an opinion that directly opposed the ideas and conclusions that Scalia had espoused so stridently in his *Webster* concurring opinion. As described in Chapter 2, one of Scalia's themes in deciding cases was an open disregard for the importance of stare decisis, or case precedent, when considering prior cases that clashed with his strongly held views about the Constitution's meaning. Scalia's *Webster* concurring opinion reinforced this disregard by calling for an immediate reversal of a precedent, *Roe*, with which Scalia strongly disagreed, despite the fact that a majority of justices had consistently reaffirmed the precedent for nearly two decades. O'Connor, Souter, and Kennedy devoted an unusually long section of their opinion to discussing the importance of stare decisis and comparing the *Roe* precedent with the Supreme Court's treatment of controversial precedents in earlier eras.[59] Few prior Supreme Court opinions have given such detailed attention to the importance of case precedent for the Supreme Court's role in the American governing system.

Lee Epstein and Joseph Kobylka have argued that "there is substantial evidence that the less ideologically driven justices take [legal] arguments seriously and account for them in explaining positions they take."[60] Because Souter and O'Connor constituted "the 'middle,' or whatever there is of a 'middle' on the strongly conservative Court,"[61] perhaps their behavior was explainable, in part, by Epstein and Kobylka's argument that decisions by less ideological justices are more likely to be influenced by legal reasoning and not by policy preferences alone.[62] But why did they find legal arguments about stare decisis so powerful in the abortion case when they actively participated in reversing precedents concerning other controversial issues, such as criminal defendants' rights? Was there a catalyst, such as Justice Scalia's outspokenness, that made them treat case precedent more seriously and respect it in accordance with traditional legal theory?

Moreover, can Justice Kennedy's switch from critic of *Roe* to defender of the *Roe* precedent possibly be explained solely in terms of his concern about legal reasoning and stare decisis? By previously joining Chief Justice Rehnquist's opinion in the *Webster* case, Justice Kennedy appeared intent upon joining efforts by Rehnquist and White to criticize *Roe*'s reasoning persuasively in order to set the stage for the dismantling of the judicial policy on abortion. He showed no concern about stare decisis in any previous abortion decision. Kennedy switched positions only after Justice Scalia attacked his conservative allies for not being forthright in their actions and after Scalia openly advocated immediate reversal for the sake of *his* vision of the Court's role in the governing system.

By pressing his views in such an open, public, and undiplomatic manner, Scalia apparently forced his colleagues to confront exactly how they wished to portray the Court's image and role. Kennedy, as well as O'Connor and Souter, suddenly evinced serious concerns about the risk that the Court's decisions on abortion would appear to be shaped by politically motivated changes in the Court's composition or by pressures from society. When confronted and forced to take a stand, Justice Kennedy opted to oppose his attacker,

Scalia, by enunciating a more traditional view of the Court's role that emphasized the importance of case precedent.

During the course of her career on the Supreme Court, Justice O'Connor moved from authoring the most systematic critique of *Roe v. Wade*'s reasoning in her dissenting opinion in the 1983 Akron case to declaring in 1992 that "*Roe* has . . . in no sense proven 'unworkable.' "[63] In the interim, Chief Justice Rehnquist and Justice White employed the traditional strategic interactions of a collegial appellate court by attempting to patiently cultivate O'Connor's support through persuasion and emphasis on their shared points of agreement.

Their attempt to encourage O'Connor to join their efforts to overturn *Roe* was hampered, if not torpedoed, by Scalia's decision to make O'Connor the focus of sustained personal attacks and public derision in his *Webster* concurring opinion. Like other justices on the Supreme Court, Justice O'Connor was a successful politician and accomplished state appellate judge before being appointed to the Supreme Court. Because of her intelligence, confidence, and record of success, O'Connor was not likely to feel persuaded to adopt Scalia's viewpoints when his means of convincing her was to implicitly accuse her in a strongly worded judicial opinion of hypocrisy, disingenuousness, and cowardice. O'Connor and her coauthors implied that they were personally opposed to abortion, but that their sense of larger obligations to the Supreme Court and to the image of law forced them to take a stand in support of stare decisis: "Some of us as individuals find abortion offensive to our most basic principles of morality, but that cannot control our decision. Our obligation is to define the liberty of all, not to mandate our own moral code."[64]

If Scalia had assisted Rehnquist and White in keeping the path clear for an incremental erosion and gradual elimination of *Roe*, Justices O'Connor and Kennedy, and perhaps even Souter, who lacked a record of opinions on the abortion issue, might have found a way to support their preferred policy outcomes. By forcing the issue in a strident and personal way, Scalia pushed his colleagues away by offending them. According to a report in the *Wall Street Journal*, Scalia's attacks affected O'Connor and Kennedy in particular: " 'There is no question that [Souter] doesn't take [criticism from Justice Scalia] as personally as Kennedy and O'Connor,' says a lawyer who clerked [during the 1991–92] term for another justice."[65] Moreover, Scalia's combative style forced his fellow conservatives to confront their fundamental fears about the Court's image and role. Thus, Scalia unintentionally contributed to the maintenance of the very precedent that he so strongly opposed and that political conservatives had long hoped the conservative Rehnquist Court would erase.

Although President Bill Clinton is likely to have the opportunity to appoint liberal Democrats to serve on the Supreme Court, he is not likely to alter quickly the numerical dominance of conservatives. Thus, even after the 1992 joint opinion reaffirming *Roe*, a hypothetical possibility existed that the conservatives could regroup and, through strategic and persuasive interactions, find common ground to induce O'Connor or Kennedy or Souter to join subsequent opinions that would further diminish the power of *Roe v. Wade*. Any regrouping of the conservatives would require that the justices who sought reversal of *Roe* manifest the same strategic patience evident in Chief Justice Rehnquist's *Webster* opinion as a means to build bridges within a conservative bloc that voted relatively cohesively in some prior terms. During the 1990 term, for example, a conservative bloc of justices, including Rehnquist, Scalia, O'Connor, Kennedy, Souter, and White, supported each other's opinions with remarkable frequency.[66] From the tone and content of Scalia's 1992 opinion on behalf of the four opponents of *Roe*, however, it appeared that any potential bridges had not merely been burned but had been destroyed with nuclear force.

In his opinion, Scalia acknowledged that O'Connor, Souter, and Kennedy had responded directly to his arguments when they wrote the joint opinion to reaffirm *Roe*: "The Court destroys the proposition, evidently meant to represent my position [on the meaning of] 'liberty.' "[67] Scalia then proceeded to rebut the joint opinion by using the unprecedented technique of highlighting in boldface type individual assertions by O'Connor, Souter, and Kennedy before critiquing each assertion in detail. As usual, Scalia employed his characteristic strong language is skewering the reasoning and conclusions of those who oppose his viewpoints:

The emptiness of the "reasoned judgment" that produced *Roe* is displayed in plain view by the fact that . . . the best the Court can do to explain how it is that the word "liberty" *must* include the right to destroy human fetuses is to rattle off a collection of adjectives that simply decorate a value judgment and conceal a political choice.[68]

He further declared that the joint authors' effort to "portray *Roe* as the statesmanlike 'settlement' of a divisive issue . . . is nothing less than Orwellian."[69] Scalia's sarcasm shone through when he accused the authors of the joint opinion of having produced a "revised fabricated version" of *Roe v. Wade*.[70] He also directed pointed criticism once again at Justice O'Connor for being inconsistent with her opinions in other cases.[71] The language that Scalia used in responding to the three coauthors' concerns about stare decisis and the Court's image was exceptionally harsh:

The Imperial Judiciary lives. It is instructive to compare this Nietzschean vision of us unelected, life-tenured judges—leading a Volk . . . whose very "belief in themselves" is mystically bound up in their "understanding" of a Court that "speak[s] before all others for their constitutional ideals"—with the somewhat more modest role envisioned for these lawyers by the Founders. . . . The only principle the Court "adheres" to, it seems to me, is the principle that the Court must be seen as standing by *Roe*. That is not a principle of law (which I thought is what the Court was talking about), but a principle of *Realpolitik*—and a wrong one at that.[72]

Ultimately, the strength of Scalia's convictions about the correct action for the Supreme Court to take concerning abortion motivated him to aim exceptionally sharp criticisms at his colleagues and thereby diminished any likelihood that his views would ever prevail.

JUDICIAL MODERATION AND CONSERVATIVE DISAPPOINTMENT

The First Amendment contains the Establishment Clause, which forbids laws "respecting an establishment of religion." Various justices have disagreed about whether this provision requires strict separation of church and state, mandates government neutrality in implementing policies that affect religions, or permits governmental accommodation and assistance for various religions.

During the tenure of Chief Justice Earl Warren, the Supreme Court acted for the first time to enforce a strict separation perspective, and in doing so, the justices collided with traditional, accepted practices that brought Christianity into contact with public institutions. Most notably, the Warren Court "unleashed a firestorm of conservative criticism"[73] in the aftermath of decisions in the 1960s that outlawed organized prayers[74] and Bible reading in public school classrooms:[75] "One newspaper headline screamed 'COURT OUTLAWS GOD.' An outraged Billy Graham thundered 'God pity our country when we can no longer appeal to God for help,' . . . Senator Sam Ervin of North Carolina charged that the Supreme Court 'made God unconstitutional.' "[76]

These adverse reactions generated political initiatives designed to test, challenge, and evade the Supreme Court's decision to withdraw organized religion from the public schools. For example, members of Congress proposed approximately 300 constitutional amendments to reverse the Supreme Court's school prayer decision in the twenty-five years after the decision.[77] States passed new laws and initiated new practices designed to challenge or evade the Supreme Court's rulings and thereby forced the Court to issue new decisions concerning religious activities within the public schools.[78] Such governmental actions created opportunities for the Supreme Court's justices to revise or alter precedents that religious interest groups and their elected representatives found to be objectionable.

When new Establishment Clause cases were presented to the high court during the Burger Court era, the Nixon appointees did not counteract the Warren Court's emphasis on strict separation of church and state. In 1971, the Court enunciated a three-prong test for Establishment Clause cases known as the "*Lemon* test" (*Lemon v. Kurtzman*), which became the fundamental method for deciding whether any situation created improper contacts between government and religion.[79] Under the *Lemon* test, in order for a challenged governmental action to survive judicial scrutiny when it implicates the Establishment Clause: "First, the statute must have a secular legislative purpose; second, its principal or primary effect must be one that neither advances nor inhibits religion . . . ; finally, the statute must not foster 'excessive entanglement with religion.' "[80] Because a statute or government program must pass all three prongs of the *Lemon* test in order to survive, it is difficult for a government policy or program to avoid invalidation when a majority of justices choose to apply the test. The test was used to strike down various state laws intended to provide financial assistance to parochial schools and those intended to return forms of prayer to the nation's public school classrooms.

Among the post-Warren Court presidents, President Reagan was unique in his outspoken desire for the Supreme Court to alter its decisions affecting religious freedom:

It took the candidacy of Ronald Reagan to bring school prayer back to the political agenda. As part of his strategy to form a new GOP coalition and to woo southern, working class, and Catholic voters, Reagan promised to actively support an amendment to the Constitution that would return prayer to the public schools. . . . Presidents Kennedy, Johnson, Nixon, Ford, and Carter either shied away from or ignored altogether the school prayer controversy. Only Ronald Reagan made school prayer a campaign pledge and supplied presidential leadership behind a constitutional amendment.[81]

Reagan and his political allies sought to replace the Warren Court's notion of strict separation of church and state with a governmental accommodation perspective on religious freedom that would permit government assistance for religious institutions and for religious programs within public schools. In his 1987 State of the Union Address, Reagan said: "Finally let's stop suppressing the spiritual core of our national being. . . . The 100th Congress of the United States should be remembered as the one that ended the expulsion of God from America's classrooms."[82] Although the Reagan administration was most concerned about appointing federal judicial officers who would reverse trends on abortion, affirmative action, and criminal defendants' rights, it was likely that many of the politically conservative lawyers who passed the necessary litmus tests in order to qualify for judicial appointment also shared or sympathized with Reagan's accommodationist views on religious freedom.

In order to advance its policy positions and take advantage of the Supreme Court's conservative moment, the Reagan administration altered the role of the Office of Solicitor General. The solicitor general, one of the most prestigious posts for lawyers, presents arguments to the Supreme Court on behalf of the federal government. Instead of maintaining the solicitor general's tradition of presenting scholarly, thoughtful, and trustworthy briefs to the Court, the Solicitor General's Office under Reagan lost some of its luster by presenting strident, partisan policy arguments. Several recent justices on the Supreme Court expressed concerns during anonymous interviews that the Solicitor General's Office under the Reagan administration had undergone a detrimental transformation.[83]

In regard to cases affecting religious freedom, the solicitor general's arguments advocating reversal of established precedents and the dismantling of the *Lemon* test found a receptive audience among the Supreme Court's emerging conservative majority. When a case arose in 1984 concerning the permissibility of a city-owned Christian nativity scene displayed in public, the Reagan administration argued that the Supreme Court should revise the *Lemon* test: "We suggest that the three-part test . . . results in analytic overkill when applied to the type of government action under consideration here."[84] A closely divided Supreme Court supported the nativity scene in a five-to-four decision, but did not formally dismantle the *Lemon* test.[85]

The Conservative Justices' Views of the Establishment Clause

In the mid-1980s, one scholar assessed the Supreme Court's Establishment Clause decisions and found the Court deeply divided between separationists and accommodationists, with a few justices in the middle casting the decisive votes in most cases: "No matter what test has been employed by the present members of the Court, Justices William J. Brennan, Thurgood Marshall, and John Paul Stevens will probably find a violation of the establishment clause, while Justices William H. Rehnquist and Byron R. White, joined by Chief Justice Warren E. Burger, will probably not find such a violation, and Justices Sandra Day O'Connor, Harry A. Blackmun, and, above all, Lewis F. Powell will hold the balance of power that determines the result."[86] After that evaluation, two Reagan appointees, Justices Scalia and Kennedy, replaced one accommodationist (Burger) and one swing voter (Powell), and Bush appointees Justices Souter and Thomas replaced two separationists (Brennan and Marshall). As a result of the changes in the Court's composition, only Justice Stevens remained as a strong separationist in the tradition of his liberal predecessors on the Warren Court.

Individual members of the Rehnquist Court appeared to be sympathetic to the conservative objective of reversing the Warren Court's efforts to require strict separation of church and state. Justice White, for example, was a long-standing critic of the Supreme Court's reasoning in Establishment Clause cases. White was the lone dissenter in *Lemon v. Kurtzman* in 1971, and he persisted in his criticisms of the *Lemon* test. In his *Lemon* dissent, White presented an accommodationist perspective that accepted state statutes providing direct financial assistance to religious schools: "That religion and private interests other than education may substantially benefit does not convert these laws into impermissible establishments of religion."[87] In White's view, legislation with a secular purpose may provide governmental aid to religion. White consistently dissented when the Court employed the *Lemon* test to strike down governmental aid to religious schools. As White noted in one dissenting opinion, "I am quite unreconciled to the Court's decision in *Lemon v. Kurtzman*. . . . I thought then, and I think now, that the Court's conclusion there was not required by the First Amendment and is contrary to the long-range interests of the country."[88]

White's views on the Establishment Clause have carried over into other religion cases. For example, when he supported Alabama's silent school prayer statute that had been struck down by a six-member majority, White endorsed Chief Justice Rehnquist's strong criticism of the *Lemon* test.[89] The majority invalidated the statute under the "purpose" prong of the *Lemon* test because Alabama legislators admitted that the statute was intended as an effort to return prayer to the public schools.[90]

Chief Justice Rehnquist consistently criticized the Supreme Court's use of the *Lemon* test. In the Alabama school prayer case, Rehnquist presented one of the strongest critiques of the *Lemon* test:

The three-part test has simply not provided adequate standards for deciding Establishment Clause cases, as this Court has slowly come to realize. Even worse, the *Lemon* test has caused this Court to fracture into unworkable plurality opinions . . . depending upon how each of the three factors applies to a certain state action.[91]

The basis for Rehnquist's disagreement with the Court's Establishment Clause decisions is his view that a government accommodation perspective provides the proper approach for interpreting the First Amendment. According to Rehnquist, the Establishment Clause was designed "to prevent the establishment of a national religion [and] the governmental preference of one religious sect over another."[92] Thus, Rehnquist is strongly critical of language in opinions that require the strict separation of church and state:

The three-part [*Lemon*] test represents a determined effort to craft a workable rule from a historically faulty doctrine; but the rule can only be as sound as the doctrine it attempts to service. . . . Our perception has been clouded not by the Constitution but by the mists of an unnecessary metaphor [concerning a "wall" of separation between church and state].[93]

Moreover, Rehnquist argues that the original intent of the Establishment Clause's framers was to permit government accommodation of religion rather than to enforce strict separation of church and state.[94] Rehnquist's interpretation of original intent has been criticized by constitutional historians,[95] but it was he, rather than they, who was in the position to define the Establishment Clause's meaning.

Not surprisingly, Chief Justice Rehnquist's disagreements with his Warren Court predecessors and Burger Court colleagues about the Establishment Clause reflect his own personal insensitivity to the need to protect religious minorities. Rehnquist's sensitivity, or lack thereof, was indicated by his sponsorship of a "Christmas party" at the Supreme Court, complete with religious music such as "Silent Night."[96] According to published notes from a daily journal kept by a student intern at the Supreme Court, "Some of the [law] clerks are really offended" because they "don't think there should be a party celebrating a clearly Christian holiday in a building that's supposed to stand by the separation of church and state. A holiday party, fine, but not a Christmas party."[97] A group of law clerks raised the issue with the chief justice, and Rehnquist "said he couldn't understand why anyone was offended, he'd had a Jewish clerk once who didn't mind."[98]

This revealing anecdote indicates that one source of Rehnquist's accommodationist perspective is his lack of understanding concerning the views of members of minority religious groups who object to being subjected to government-sponsored Christian programs. Most revealing of all, perhaps, is Rehnquist's justification for the Christmas party based on one Jewish law clerk's failure to object to the practice. There is reason to doubt that a single law clerk would necessarily challenge the Chief Justice of the United States within the organizational hierarchy of the Supreme Court in which the law clerk was obligated to work closely for and please the Chief Justice. Moreover, Rehnquist's troubling insensitivity to minority concerns seems clearly revealed by his belief that one individual's failure to raise objections somehow constitutes endorsement and acceptance on behalf of all non-Christians.

Scholars took note of Justice Kennedy's accommodationist views after only a few terms on the Court.[99] In Kennedy's first two opinions in religious freedom cases, both concerning the Establishment Clause, he advanced his accommodationist perspective strongly.[100] In his most strident opinion, Justice Kennedy, joined by Rehnquist, Scalia, and White, accused the Court majority of harboring "an unjustified hostility toward religion" because it applied the *Lemon* test to forbid the display of a nativity scene in a county courthouse.[101] In this case and a prior case concerning government-sponsored displays of religious symbols during the Christmas season, the Court required that the religious symbols be joined by nonreligious symbols, such as Christmas trees, reindeer, and snowmen, in order to "secularize" the holiday display.[102] Justice Kennedy joined Rehnquist, Scalia, and White in opposing such limitations and in endorsing greater government support and accommodation for religious programs.

The orientation of Justice Kennedy toward minority religious groups was indicated by Kennedy's opinion in the case concerning religious holiday displays in public buildings.[103] Because a five-member majority (Brennan, Marshall, Stevens, Blackmun, and O'Connor) applied the *Lemon* test and thereby declined to accept the conservatives' accommodationist perspective, Kennedy complained in dissent that the Christian majority was being victimized by the Supreme Court:

I am quite certain that ["the reasonable person"] will take away a salient message from our holding in this case: the Supreme Court of the United States has concluded that the First Amendment creates classes of religions based on the relative number of adherents. Those religions enjoying the largest following must be consigned to the status of least-favored faiths so as to avoid any possible risk of offending members of minority religions.[104]

From the perspective of conservative, accommodationist justices, if the Christian majority cannot have its way in gaining government support for religious programs and displays, Christians are thereby victimized by discriminatory treatment. The accommodationist viewpoint that underlies this statement appeared incapable of recognizing or accepting that the government might be neutral and thereby not favor any religious group. The implicit message in this statement—namely that "we are the majority; therefore, we must have our way"—seemed to epitomize an orientation toward religious freedom that lacks sensitivity to the concerns and rights of members of religious minorities.

Justice O'Connor agreed with the other members of the emerging conservative majority concerning the appropriate outcomes in two thirds or more of all religious freedom cases.[105] In Establishment Clause cases, O'Connor dissented from decisions that applied the *Lemon* test to find that the government had improperly aided religious schools. O'Connor strongly criticized the Court's application of the *Lemon* test. She "question[s] the utility of [the 'excessive entanglement' prong] as a separate Establishment Clause standard in most cases" because it may wrongly "[condemn] benign cooperation between church and state."[106] She has also indicated her dissatisfaction with the "purpose" prong of the *Lemon* test as it has been applied by the Supreme Court.[107]

In addition to her criticisms of the strict separation approach to the First Amendment taken by the Warren Court and Burger Court–era justices, Justice O'Connor indicated that she does not possess her predecessors' concern for the protection of religious minorities. Such concerns among Warren Court justices generated several important decisions concerning strict separation. Justice O'Connor ignited an embarrassing controversy when she received a request from conservative Republican leaders in Arizona to provide authoritative case citations that would justify the politicians' claim that the United States is a "Christian nation . . . based on the absolute law of the Bible."[108] O'Connor, a former Republican state senator in Arizona, complied with the request, and her letter, which was written on Supreme Court stationary, was used in the annual state party convention to support the successful adoption of a resolution proclaiming the "Christian" character of the country.[109]

O'Connor claimed that she regretted that a letter written to a private acquaintance had been used for political purposes, yet the original request she received specifically asked for her help in securing passage of a politically motivated proclamation. The request to O'Connor stated: "Republicans are making some interesting advances in this heavily controlled Democratic area. Some of us are proposing a resolution which acknowledges that the Supreme Court ruled in 1892 that this is a Christian Nation. It would be beneficial and interesting to have a letter from you . . . "[110] Unfortunately, O'Connor stretched so far in attempting to fulfill this request that, in addition to the outdated 1892 case that was written before the development of religious freedom jurisprudence,[111] she included two additional case citations that do not support the assertion that the United States is a "Christian nation."[112]

The viewpoints of Rehnquist, White, Kennedy, and O'Connor contributed to the development of a conservative moment of opportunity to reshape the meaning of the Establishment Clause. The moment of opportunity was reinforced by the strong views of Justice Scalia, who, not surprisingly, was even more outspoken than several of his conservative colleagues in his opposition to the judicial policy of strict separation of church and state. In religious freedom cases, Scalia's strident views led him to criticize the *Lemon* test sharply in Establishment Clause cases and to limit the scope of Free Exercise Clause claims that collide with governmental actions.

In a case in which a seven-to-two majority on the Court invalidated a Louisiana law requiring the teaching of "creation science" along with evolution in public schools, Scalia's dissenting opinion, joined by Chief Justice Rehnquist, argued that the Court had improperly asserted that the Louisiana statute lacked a secular purpose.[113] The majority had invalidated the statute under the "purpose" prong of the *Lemon* test by finding that "[t]he preeminent purpose of the Louisiana Legislature was clearly to advance the religious viewpoint that a supernatural being created mankind."[114] Scalia criticized both the existence and use of the *Lemon* test: "I doubt whether the 'purpose' requirement of *Lemon* is a proper interpretation of the Constitution; but even if it were, I could not agree with the Court's assessment that the requirement was not satisfied here."[115] Scalia argued that it should not matter if legislators have a religious purpose in enacting a statute or if the statute happened to coincide with the legislators' religious beliefs as long as there was also some secular purpose.[116] Scalia, like Rehnquist, prefers to defer to the actions of elected officials if possible and therefore is reluctant to endorse assertions of individuals' constitutional rights that would invalidate legislative or executive branch actions. Scalia's opinion in the case concluded with one of the strongest calls yet for the dismantling of the *Lemon* test:

In the past we have attempted to justify our embarrassing Establishment Clause jurisprudence on the ground that it "sacrifices clarity and predictability for flexibility." . . . Abandoning *Lemon*'s purpose test—a test which exacerbates the tension between the Free Exercise and Establishment Clauses, has no basis in the language or history of the Amendment, and, as today's decision shows, has wonderfully flexible consequences—would be a good place to start.[117]

In a subsequent dissenting opinion, joined by Chief Justice Rehnquist and Justice Kennedy, Scalia enunciated his accommodationist perspective more explicitly.[118] He used his characteristic strong language and sarcasm to criticize the majority's decision to invalidate a Texas statute that exempted religious periodicals from the state sales tax:

As a judicial demolition project, today's decision is impressive. The machinery employed by the opinions of Justice BRENNAN and Justice BLACKMUN is no more substantial than the antinomy that accommodation of religion may be required but is not permitted, and the bold but unsupportable assertion (given such realities as the text of the Declaration of Independence, the national Thanksgiving Day proclaimed by every President since Lincoln, the inscriptions on our coins, the words of our Pledge of Allegiance, the invocation with which sessions of our Court are opened and, come to think of it, the discriminatory protection of freedom of religion in the Constitution) that government may not "convey a message of endorsement of religion."[119]

Prayers at Public School Graduations

Political conservatives saw a golden moment of opportunity appear during the 1991 term when the Supreme Court agreed to hear a case challenging the reading of prayers by clergy at public school graduations. Because the Rehnquist Court contained five Reagan and Bush appointees in addition to two other primary critics of liberal Establishment Clause jurisprudence, Chief Justice Rehnquist and Justice White, it appeared that the Court might be positioned to reverse or substantially modify the controversial Warren Court–era decisions forbidding school prayer and other forms of government support for religion. Ultimately, however, the political conservatives were deeply disappointed because, as in the 1992 abortion case, Justices Kennedy, O'Connor, and Souter joined the two most liberal justices, Burger Court holdovers Blackmun and Stevens, to reaffirm and, in fact, broaden the judicial ban on public school prayer. In an opinion by Justice Kennedy, the Court extended the prohibition on public school prayer to cover graduation ceremonies as well as classroom situations.[120]

The participation of conservative justices, and especially Justice Kennedy, in the broadening of a controversial liberal judicial policy initiated in the Warren Court era appears puzzling at first glance. Justice O'Connor had criticized strict separation doctrines and advocated that states be permitted to provide financial assistance to parochial schools. Justice Kennedy had previously been a consistent ally of Rehnquist, Scalia, and White when they advocated a government accommodation perspective in Establishment Clause cases. Viewed in isolation, the liberal outcome in the prayer decision seems to reflect inconsistency or changed viewpoints on the part of key conservatives. However, it must be remembered that the prayer case was decided during the very same term as the abortion case in which Scalia had inadvertently driven Kennedy, O'Connor, and Souter away from their usual conservative allies.

Just as the prospect of reversing *Roe v. Wade* made the three justices concerned about the need to protect the Court's image by respecting stare decisis, any major change in Establishment Clause jurisprudence in the graduation prayer case would have required alteration of precedents even older than *Roe*. In the abortion case, the coauthored opinion explained the three justices' concerns at length. In the prayer case, Justice Souter's concurring opinion, joined by Justices O'Connor and Stevens, raised this concern, albeit in a less extensive discussion, by concluding that accommodationist arguments about the original intent of the First Amendment were not sufficiently persuasive to justify "rais[ing] a threat to *stare decisis*."[121]

Given that Kennedy, O'Connor, and Souter were about to issue an extensive defense of stare decisis in order to respond to Scalia in the abortion case, they could not very well participate in the reversal of even older precedents concerning the Establishment Clause. Scalia was always ready to use his sharp pen to pounce on those who disagree with him, especially Justice O'Connor, when he perceived that their opinions concerning stare decisis and other jurisprudential issues were inconsistent. Any decision other than reaffirmation of strict separation by O'Connor, Kennedy, and Souter would have given Scalia more ammunition to throw against them in the abortion case.

Individual cases and issues are not decided in isolation by the justices. During the course of any term, justices are simultaneously drafting and circulating opinions concerning a variety of pending cases that must be decided by the end of each annual term in June. O'Connor, Souter, and Kennedy spent several months during spring 1992 drafting an opinion concerning abortion that they knew was anxiously awaited by the entire nation and was certain to cause controversy by disappointing and enraging antiabortion activists and political conservatives in the Republican party. The effort and care that they directed at an opinion that caused Justice Scalia to comment on "[i]ts length and what might be called its epic tone"[122] undoubtedly made them very conscious of what they were saying in opinions while simultaneously deciding other pending cases. Thus, Scalia's powerful impact on the abortion issue by inadvertently contributing to the defeat of a primary conservative policy objective, namely the overturning of *Roe*, carried over into the school prayer case because that case implicated the same jurisprudential issue (i.e., stare decisis) that was central to the counterarguments directed at Scalia in the abortion case. When Scalia's judicial behavior and the tone of his opinions pushed his conservative allies away in the abortion case, they needed to stay away from Scalia in other cases, too, in order to maintain an image of consistency.

NOTES

1. David Kaplan and Bob Cohn, "The Court's Mr. Right," *Newsweek*, 5 November 1990, p. 62.

2. United States v. Leon, 468 U.S. 897, 922 (1984).

3. Texas v. Johnson, 109 S. Ct. 2533 (1989); United States v. Eichman, 110 S. Ct. 2404 (1990).

4. Weeks v. United States, 232 U.S. 383 (1914).

5. Barron v. Baltimore, 7 Peters 243 (1833).

6. Gitlow v. New York, 268 U.S. 652 (1925).

7. Near v. Minnesota, 283 U.S. 697 (1931).

8. Wolf v. Colorado, 338 U.S. 25 (1949).

9. Rochin v. California, 3342 U.S. 165 (1952).

10. Mapp v. Ohio, 367 U.S. 643 (1961).

11. Peter F. Nardulli, "The Societal Costs of the Exclusionary Rule: An Empirical Assessment," *American Bar Foundation Research Journal* (1983): 585–690; Thomas Y. Davies, "A Hard Look at What We Know (and Still Need to Learn) About the 'Costs' of the Exclusionary Rule: The NIJ Study and Other Studies of 'Lost' Arrests," *American Bar Foundation Research Journal* (1983): 611–690.

12. Bivens v. Six Unknown Named Agents of the Federal Bureau of Narcotics, 403 U.S. 388, 421–427 (1971) (Burger, C.J., dissenting).

13. Nix v. Williams, 467 U.S. 431 (1984).

14. United States v. Leon, 468 U.S. 897 (1984).

15. New York v. Quarles, 467 U.S. 649 (1984).

16. Lincoln Caplan, *The Tenth Justice: The Solicitor General and the Rule of Law* (New York: Random House, 1987), pp. 119–121.

17. Arizona v. Hicks, 107 S. Ct. 1149 (1987).

18. Ibid., p. 1152.

19. Coolidge v. New Hampshire, 403 U.S. 433, 465–471 (1971).

20. Arizona v. Hicks, 107 S. Ct. 1149, 1157 (O'Connor, J., dissenting).

21. Ibid., p. 1152.

22. Ibid., p. 1155.

23. Sheldon Goldman, *Constitutional Law: Cases and Essays*, 2nd ed. (New York: HarperCollins, 1991), p. 588.

24. Illinois v. Krull, 480 U.S. 340 (1987); O'Connor v. Ortega, 480 U.S. 709 (1987).

25. Christopher E. Smith, "Bright-Line Rules and the Supreme Court: The Tension between Clarity in Legal Doctrine and Justices' Policy Preferences," *Ohio Northern University Law Review* 16 (1989): 131–133.

26. Joyce Baugh, "Justice Antonin Scalia and the Freshman Effect," paper presented at the annual meeting of the Midwest Political Science Association, April 1989, p. 18.

27. Christopher E. Smith, "Justice Antonin Scalia and Criminal Justice Cases," *Kentucky Law Journal* 81 (1992–93): 193.

28. Roe v. Wade, 410 U.S. 113 (1973).

29. See Patricia G. Steinhoff and Milton Diamond, *Abortion Politics: The Hawaii Experience* (Honolulu: University Press of Hawaii, 1977).

30. Roe v. Wade, 410 U.S. 113 (1973).

31. Griswold v. Connecticut, 381 U.S. 479 (1965).

32. Raymond Tatalovich and Byron W. Daynes, *The Politics of Abortion: A Study in Community Conflict in Public Policymaking* (New York: Praeger, 1981), p. 154.

33. Stephen L. Wasby, *The Supreme Court in the Federal Judicial System*, 3rd ed. (Chicago: Nelson-Hall, 1988), pp. 308–309.

34. Harris v. McRae, 448 U.S. 297 (1980).

35. Williams v. Zbaraz, 448 U.S. 358 (1980).

36. Louis Fisher, *American Constitutional Law* (New York: McGraw-Hill, 1990), p. 1150.

37. City of Akron v. Akron Center for Reproductive Health, 103 S. Ct. 2481, 2489 n. 5 (1983).

38. Roe v. Wade, 410 U.S. 113, 159 (1973).

39. See, for example, Thornburgh v. American College of Obstetricians and Gynecologists, 476 U.S. 747 (1986).

40. City of Akron v. Akron Center for Reproductive Health, 103 S. Ct. 2481, 2504–2505 (1983) (O'Connor, J., dissenting), quoting Plyler v. Doe, 457 U.S. 202, 242 (1982) (Burger, C.J., dissenting).

41. Ibid., p. 2505.

42. Antonin Scalia, "The Disease as Cure," *Washington University Law Quarterly* (1979): 153.

43. Webster v. Reproductive Health Services, 109 S. Ct. 3040 (1989).

44. Ibid., p. 3047.

45. Ibid., p. 3060 (O'Connor, J., concurring in part and concurring in judgment).

46. Ibid., p. 3063.

47. Ibid., p. 3058.

48. Ibid.

49. Ibid., p. 3057.

50. Ibid., p. 3064 (Scalia, J., concurring in part and concurring in judgment).

51. Ibid.

52. Ibid.

53. Ibid., p. 3065.

54. Ibid., p. 3067.

55. Christopher E. Smith and Scott Patrick Johnson, "The First-Term Performance of Justice Clarence Thomas," *Judicature* 76 (1993): 172–178.

56. Planned Parenthood v. Casey, 112 S. Ct. 2791 (1992).

57. Ibid., p. 2814.

58. Ibid., p. 2816.

59. Ibid., pp. 2812–2816.

60. Lee Epstein and Joseph Kobylka, *The Supreme Court and Legal Change* (Chapel Hill: University of North Carolina Press, 1992), p. 310.

61. Scott P. Johnson and Christopher E. Smith, "David Souter's First Term on the Supreme Court: The Impact of a New Justice," *Judicature* 75 (1992): 240.

62. Epstein and Kobylka, p. 310.

63. Planned Parenthood v. Casey, 122 S. Ct. 2791, p. 2809 (1992).

64. Ibid., p. 2807.

65. Paul M. Barrett, "Independent Justice: David Souter Emerges as Reflective Moderate on the Supreme Court," *Wall Street Journal*, 2 February 1993, pp. A1, A6.

66. Johnson and Smith, p. 239.

67. Planned Parenthood v. Casey, 112 S. Ct. 2791, 2874 (1992) (Scalia, J., concurring in judgment in part and dissenting in part).

68. Ibid., p. 2875.

69. Ibid., p. 2882.

70. Ibid., p. 2876.

71. Ibid., pp. 2878–2879.

72. Ibid., pp. 2882–2883.

73. Melvin I. Urofsky, *The Continuity of Change: The Supreme Court and Individual Liberties, 1953–1986* (Belmont, Calif.: Wadsworth, 1991), p. 33.

74. Engel v. Vitale, 370 U.S. 421 (1962).

75. Abington School District v. Schempp, 374 U.S. 203 (1963).

76. Urofsky, p. 33.

77. Henry Abraham, *Freedom and the Court*, 5th ed. (New York: Oxford University Press, 1988), p. 337.

78. See Board of Education of Netcong v. State Board of Education, 401 U.S. 1013 (1971) (public schools cannot utilize prayers printed in the *Congressional Record* in order to institute daily religious observance); Stone v. Graham, 449 U.S. 39 (1980) (state may not require that privately purchased copies of the Ten Commandments be posted in every public school classroom).

79. Lemon v. Kurtzman, 403 U.S. 602 (1971).

80. Ibid., pp. 612–613.

81. John A. Murley, "School Prayer: Free Exercise of Religion or Establishment of Religion?" in *Social Regulatory Policy: Moral Controversies in American Politics*, eds. Raymond Tatolovich and Byron Daynes (Boulder, Colo: Westview Press, 1988), pp. 33–34.

82. Ibid., p. 34.

83. Caplan, pp. 253, 264–267.

84. Ibid., p. 96.

85. Lynch v. Donnelly, 465 U.S. 668 (1984).

86. Leonard Levy, *The Establishment Clause: Religion and the First Amendment* (New York: Macmillan, 1986), pp. 129–130.

87. Lemon v. Kurtzman, 94 S. Ct. 2135, 2137 (1971) (White, J., dissenting).

88. Committee for Public Education & Religious Liberty v. Nyquist, 93 S. Ct. 2993, 2996 (1973) (White, J., dissenting).

89. Wallace v. Jaffree, 472 U.S. 38, 90 (1985) (White, J., dissenting).

90. Wallace v. Jaffree, 472 U.S. 38, 57–60 (1985).

91. Wallace v. Jaffree, 472 U.S. 38, 110 (1985) (Rehnquist, C.J., dissenting).

92. Ibid., p. 100.

93. Ibid., pp. 110, 112.

94. Ibid., pp. 110, 113.

95. Levy, pp. xii–xiii.

96. Joyce O'Connor, "Selections from Notes Kept on an Internship at the U.S. Supreme Court, Fall 1988," *Law, Courts, and Judicial Process Section Newsletter* 6 (Spring 1989): 40, 45–46.

97. Ibid., p. 45.

98. Ibid.

99. Jack Peltason, *Corwin & Peltason's Understanding the Constitution*, 12th ed. (New York: Harcourt Brace Jovanovich, 1991), p. 172.

100. See Bowen v. Kendrick, 108 S. Ct. 2562, 2582 (1988) (Kennedy, J., concurring).

101. County of Allegheny v. American Civil Liberties Union, 109 S. Ct. 3086, 3134 (Kennedy, J., concurring in judgment in part and dissenting in part).

102. Lynch v. Donnelly, 104 S. Ct. 1355, 1358, 1363 (1984).

103. County of Allegheny v. American Civil Liberties Union, 109 S. Ct. 3086 (1989).

104. County of Allegheny v. American Civil Liberties Union, 109 S. Ct. at 3145 (Kennedy, J., concurring in judgment in part and dissenting in part).

105. Christopher E. Smith and Linda Fry, "Vigilance or Accommodation: The Changing Supreme Court and Religious Freedom," *Syracuse Law Review* 42 (1991): 917.

106. Aguilar v. Felton, 105 S. Ct. 3232, 3243 (1985) (O'Connor, J., dissenting).

107. Lynch v. Donnelly, 104 S. Ct. 1355, 1365–1369 (1984) (O'Connor, J., concurring).

108. Alan Dershowitz, "Justice O'Connor's Second Indiscretion," *New York Times*, 2 April 1989, p. 31.

109. "A Private Opinion," *Time*, 27 March 1989, p. 45.

110. Dershowitz, p. 31.

111. Church of the Holy Trinity v. United States, 143 U.S. 457 (1892).

112. Zorach v. Clauson, 343 U.S. 306 (1952); McGowan v. Maryland, 366 U.S. 420 (1961).

113. Edwards v. Aguillard, 107 S. Ct. 2573, 2593 (1987) (Scalia, J., dissenting).

114. Edwards v. Aguillard, 107 S. Ct. at 2581.

115. Edwards v. Aguillard, 107 S. Ct. at 2593 (Scalia, J., dissenting).

116. Ibid., pp. 2594–2595.

117. Ibid., p. 2607.

118. Texas Monthly, Inc. v. Bullock, 109 S. Ct. 890, 907 (1989) (Scalia, J., dissenting).

119. Ibid.

120. Lee v. Weisman, 112 S. Ct. 2649 (1992).

121. Ibid., p. 2673 (Souter, J., concurring).

122. Planned Parenthood v. Casey, 112 S. Ct. 2791, 2885 (1992) (Scalia, J., concurring in judgment in part and dissenting in part).

5

The Influence of the Individual Justice

Scholars face a daunting task when attempting to analyze precisely the roles and influence of individual justices on the Supreme Court. Although the individual decision makers on the high court—unlike decision makers in larger, bureaucratic institutions—are few in number and therefore identifiable, the secretive traditions of the judicial branch impede accurate assessments of many aspects of justices' behavior. The justices' discussions with each other are secret, except on the infrequent occasions when law clerks leak information to the press, and the justices rarely agree to be interviewed by scholars or the news media. Because the Supreme Court is not accessible to scholars who wish to examine in detail the justices' attitudes and decision-making behavior, the analysis in this book, like other books on Supreme Court decision-making processes, necessarily relies on the interpretation of developments in justices' opinions, justices' voting patterns, and anecdotal information reported by scholars and the news media. Interpretive works of this sort, despite their prevalence in the field of Supreme Court politics and constitutional law, inevitably generate debates among scholars about whether the evidence relied upon actually supports an author's asserted conclusions.

ASSESSING THE INFLUENCE OF JUSTICE SCALIA

Did Justice Scalia make a fundamental contribution to the Rehnquist-era conservatives' failure to reverse key judicial policies established during the Warren and Burger Court eras? Let the debate commence. Admittedly, outside observers cannot conclude with certainty precisely what motivations spurred, for example, Justices O'Connor, Kennedy, and Souter to part company with Scalia in important cases concerning abortion and school prayer in 1992. As the preceding chapters of this book have discussed in detail, the failure of the Court's conservatives to unite on specific issues appears closely linked to Scalia's unique judicial behavior, especially his strident, sarcastic opinions and the self-righteous confidence of his strongly held, individualistic views on interpreting the Constitution. Although this development had a significant impact on conservatives' judicial policy goals concerning the important issues of abortion and school prayer, Scalia's adverse impact on his conservative colleagues was not limited to those issues.

For example, in a 1991 case, Scalia sought to redefine—or in his colleagues' view, obliterate—constitutional jurisprudence concerning the proportionality principle underlying the Eighth Amendment prohibition on "cruel and unusual punishments."[1] A five-member majority on the Court supported Michigan's mandatory life-without-parole sentence for possessing more than 650 grams of cocaine, but only Chief Justice Rehnquist adopted all of Scalia's reasoning. As the *Wall Street Journal* observed, Scalia's "argument drove off Justices O'Connor, Anthony Kennedy, and David Souter, who all voted to uphold Mr. Harmelin's sentence, but couldn't abide junking the proportionality principle."[2]

In a precursor to developments concerning abortion and school prayer in 1992, Justice Kennedy wrote a concurring opinion joined by Souter and O'Connor in which he emphasized that "*stare decisis* counsels our adherence to the narrow proportionality principle that has existed in our Eighth Amendment jurisprudence for 80 years."[3] Scalia's strident advocacy of a rigid new position caused his conservative colleagues to part company with his reasoning, but the division had little impact and attracted minimal attention because all of the conservatives still agreed on the outcome of the case. In 1992, however, the divisions among the conservatives effectively blocked the attainment of political conservatives' judicial policy goals.

The conclusion that Scalia adversely affected his own goals by his unwillingness to participate in the usual interactive processes of a collegial court has its foundations in the recognition that justices on the Supreme Court are human beings rather than legal titans on Mount Olympus. Political science research over several decades has revealed the human, political elements that affect judicial decision making by Supreme Court justices.[4] Because scholars can employ empirical methods to show that justices' policy preferences and political attitudes shape their decisions and that justices' strategic interactions shape the formation of majority voting coalitions, it makes little sense to be preoccupied with the substantive content of justices' opinions without looking closely at the human beings behind those opinions. Legal scholars may examine Justice Scalia's role on the Supreme Court by focusing solely on his strident opinions, but a more comprehensive assessment of Scalia must include analysis of his colleagues' reactions to those opinions and to the other aspects of Scalia's behavior on the Court.

Although this book has argued that Justice Scalia's opinions and behavior disrupted Republican politicians' aspirations for a cohesive, conservative Court that would counteract Warren Court jurisprudential trends, the complex nature of Supreme Court decision making makes its unwise to seek simple, reductionist explanations for judicial phenomena. Justice Scalia influenced important developments, as evidenced by his colleagues' direct responses to his strong arguments against *Roe v. Wade*, but he was not the sole cause of Supreme Court decisions that disappointed political conservatives.

Although Scalia played a pivotal role in generating adverse reactions from Justices Kennedy, O'Connor, and Souter, they undoubtedly took various other factors into consideration in making their decisions. As Lee Epstein and Joseph Kobylka observed about the Supreme Court, decision making by justices "occurs in a matrix rife with complexity. A stunning and, in some cases, analytically numbing array of forces press contemporaneously on the justices as they work in controversial areas of law."[5]

Justice Souter, for example, unlike his colleagues O'Connor and Kennedy, had never before participated in a decision concerning state regulation of abortion. He had supported federal regulations that limited the availability of abortion counseling for the poor,[6] but his views on abortion were not known when he coauthored the opinion reaffirming *Roe* in the 1992 Pennsylvania case.[7] In making his first public pronouncement about the controversial issue of abortion, he undoubtedly considered more factors than simply Justice Scalia's attacks on O'Connor, on the other conservatives, and on the concept of stare decisis.

Other justices were also undoubtedly affected by a variety of influences. Justice Kennedy, as well as Justice Scalia, manifested visible discomfort with the arguments put forward in the school prayer case[8] even before the Court discussed either that case or the Pennsylvania abortion case. According to the *New York Times* description of oral arguments, the two conservative justices were "visibly troubled" by the school board's argument that the Establishment Clause, properly understood, permitted the federal government to adopt an official national religion as long as it did not coerce people to join the religion.[9] Kennedy and Scalia appeared disturbed "at the prospect that [the school board lawyer's] vision might indeed be the logical stopping point on the journey [to undo the *Lemon* test] which [the conservative justices] had embarked."[10]

The recognition that Justice Scalia was not the sole cause of developments in the Rehnquist Court does not refute the notion that Scalia was a pivotal influence. Perhaps, for example, Kennedy suddenly recognized that the conservative justices' efforts to change the Establishment Clause had raised religious fundamentalists' hopes for an extreme form of governmental accommodation, such as the adoption of a national religion. If so, then surely the stridency of Justice Scalia, who sided with the school board without adopting all of its arguments, reinforced Kennedy's fears about how close the Court was moving toward drastically changing the meaning of the Establishment Clause. Moreover, as discussed in Chapter 4, Kennedy's simultaneous disagreement with Scalia about the importance of stare decisis for constitutional law concerning abortion policy served as an additional reminder of the risks posed by pursuit of Scalia's goals and by agreement with Scalia's reasoning. Because Scalia's influence occurred in conjunction with other developments, conclusions about the importance of Scalia's impact would be undercut if any other developments, especially those occurring during the pivotal 1991–92 term, had a greater effect than he did on the Court's key decisions.

Justice Scalia, Justice Thomas, and the 1991 Term

The 1991 Supreme Court term was the pivotal year for the political conservatives' lost moment of opportunity for reversing liberal judicial policies on abortion and school prayer. Prior to 1991, it appeared that Justice Kennedy, in particular, was a dependable ally to conservatives such as Scalia, Rehnquist, and White who wished to change the Warren Court and Burger Court precedents affecting these issues. Kennedy's 1992 decisions concerning abortion and school prayer surprised commentators because they were inconsistent with his previous decisions on those very issues.

I have argued elsewhere that Kennedy's actions in 1992 represented a dramatic departure from his prior judicial behavior.[11] Moreover, in seeking an explanation for Kennedy's changed decision-making behavior, the obvious difference between the 1991–92 term and previous terms was the presence of Clarence Thomas on the Supreme Court as a freshman justice. For several reasons, Thomas's presence on the Court could have jarred Kennedy into substantially re-evaluating how he would decide the issues of abortion and school prayer. Because Thomas immediately became such a close voting ally of Scalia and Rehnquist,[12] his certain vote to reverse *Roe* and to change Establishment Clause precedents may have forced Kennedy, as well as O'Connor and Souter, to really confront their own views about the consequences of reversing established precedents. As described in one news magazine, "Kennedy may indeed have disparaged *Roe* three years ago [in 1989], before Clarence Thomas replaced Thurgood Marshall. But faced with the possibility that *Roe* might really be overturned—and the social tumult that would ensue—[Kennedy] instinctively pulled back from the brink."[13]

In addition, some justices may have separated themselves from Thomas in subtle or even unconscious ways because of their annoyance at Thomas for several reasons. According to journalistic accounts of Thomas's confirmation proceedings, he "infuriated some, if not all, of the justices" by staging a large celebration and insisting that he be sworn in as a justice on the day after the funeral for Chief Justice Rehnquist's wife.[14]

Thomas also appeared with his wife on the cover of *People* magazine with an accompanying article in which Virginia Thomas described the confirmation hearings as "spiritual warfare. Good versus evil."[15] The article, which included a "candid" photograph of the couple reading the Bible together, was an unusually blatant attempt to rehabilitate Thomas's public image after the bruising confirmation battle and the controversy surrounding allegations of sexual harassment raised by his former assistant, Anita Hill.[16] Thomas's agreeing to do the article was exceptionally unusual because Supreme Court justices almost never appear in popular magazines except in their roles as justices to discuss, for example, the importance of the Bill of Rights. Thomas's apparently calculated effort to pander to segments of the American public did not fit with his colleagues' expectations that a Supreme Court justice remain aloof from public controversy: "The *People* magazine piece, according to Court insiders, was greeted with abject horror in the chambers of many of the justices and it brought the Court down to a different level as did the charges against Thomas."[17]

Moreover, according to a national news magazine, "two conservative justices who watched the [confirmation] hearings told their clerks that they thought Thomas lied to the Judiciary Committee."[18] Thus, in addition to his concerns about the Court's legitimacy from stable decisions, Kennedy may have moved away from his expected association with Thomas's conservative positions because of personal discomfort or concern about Thomas's adverse impact on the high court's image.

Furthermore, Thomas's votes, especially in the abortion and prayer cases, seemed to contradict his testimony during the confirmation hearings. Thomas's confirmation hearing testimony before the Senate Judiciary Committee was premised on the theme that he had not thought deeply about, and therefore had not prejudged, controversial issues, including those that had been the subject of his public speeches while working within the Reagan administration.[19] His claims that, for example, he had never discussed the abortion issue underlying *Roe v. Wade* with anyone in the eighteen years after its pronouncement were greeted with deep skepticism by critics. Because Thomas was so explicitly assertive in the opinions that he wrote and implicitly assertive by endorsing strident language in the opinions that he joined, especially the ones authored by Justice Scalia, he did little to diminish this skepticism about his veracity during the confirmation process. Thomas's conservative vote in the prayer case also appeared to directly contradict his statements during the confirmation hearings. In front of the Judiciary Committee, Thomas had said that it is wrong for government to convey the impression of endorsing particular religions and thereby make religious minority group members feel excluded.[20]

The foregoing observations about Thomas's role in defeating political conservatives' policy goals during the 1991 term do not conflict with the argument that Justice Scalia had a pivotal role in contributing to the failure of the conservative moment of opportunity. Because of the close decision-making relationship between Thomas and Scalia, it is difficult to say that any influence of Thomas's conservative voting behavior on Kennedy, O'Connor, and Souter is entirely separable from the impact of Scalia's judicial behavior upon those three justices. During his first term on the Court in 1991–92, as Thomas proved himself to be a strident conservative, his agreement rate with the outspoken Scalia in nonunanimous cases (78.9 percent) was the highest between any two justices on the Court.[21]

In addition, Thomas's opinions manifested the strident, caustic style that was characteristic of Scalia. According to one commentator, "Thomas can write in language that brings to mind Scalia's occasional let's-you-and-me-scrap tone."[22] Early in the 1991–92 term, the national news media noted that Scalia and Thomas cast identical votes in the first thirteen cases in which Thomas participated,[23] including a controversial case in which Thomas and Scalia were the only dissenters when the other seven justices identified a constitutional violation in the beating of a prisoner by correctional officers.[24] Media speculation focused on indirect influence by Scalia over Thomas through a former Scalia law clerk who clerked for Thomas during the new justice's first term on the Court.[25] Law clerks frequently write the initial draft opinions that are edited and revised into final form by the justices. According to the *Wall Street Journal*, "Justice Thomas has surrounded himself with the most conservative group of clerks at the high court, and the unvarnished rhetoric of their drafts gives his opinions a blunt tone."[26] In sum, Thomas's judicial behavior that contributed to moves toward moderation by Kennedy and the attendant defeat of the conservative moment of opportunity may have either enhanced the effects of Scalia's similar, preexisting behavior or stemmed from Scalia's influence over Thomas.

Moreover, from an alternative perspective, the impact of Scalia and Thomas can be roughly analogized to the tort law concepts of "cause in fact" and "proximate cause." These terms, albeit applied in more precise fashion, involve considerations of causation in deciding whether negligent actions damaged persons or property. Scalia's judicial behavior over several terms involved strident attacks on colleagues, sarcasm, and otherwise individualistic and irritating behavior that was inconsistent with strategic interactive processes on a collegial Court. Thus, Scalia served as the "cause in fact" of the unsuccessful conservative moment of opportunity. In other words, but for Scalia's judicial behavior, the moment may not have been lost. Thomas's behavior also apparently contributed to the lost opportunity. Thomas's presence and voting behavior on the Court during his first term may have been a "proximate cause" or an immediate catalyst for an outcome (i.e., the lost moment of opportunity) that had been set in motion and probably made inevitable by Scalia's actions over the preceding terms.

INDIVIDUAL JUSTICES AND THE FUTURE OF THE REHNQUIST COURT

Because the Supreme Court consists of only nine justices, each individual justice has the potential to have significant influence over the development of law and public policy. A justice's greatest potential for immediate impact on case outcomes will come at moments when the Court is deeply divided over the issues facing it in a given term. The Court's 1990–91 term presented just such a situation when Justice

David Souter joined the Court. As a result, Souter cast the decisive fifth vote that determined judicial outcomes for eleven cases, including seven criminal justice cases and two First Amendment cases.[27] In each instance, it appeared that Souter's conservative orientation produced outcomes that were the opposite of those that would have been generated if Souter's predecessor, legendary liberal Justice William Brennan, had remained on the Court for an additional term. This form of individual influence is visible to observers who keep track of the Supreme Court's voting patterns and the performance of each justice in joining majority or dissenting opinions concerning particular cases.

A second means through which individual justices influence the Supreme Court is the authorship of persuasive opinions. Specific opinions (and their authors) stand out for their breadth of impact on constitutional law issues and public policy. Even when a justice is not presenting the Court's decision on a case, that justice may have influence through concurring or dissenting opinions that persuade colleagues or subsequent appointees to apply the justice's reasoning in future cases. In his dissenting opinions, the first Justice John Harlan, who served during the late nineteenth century, espoused ideas about expanding the scope of civil liberties protections for individuals and about providing legal equality for African-Americans. Long after his death, his words were quoted prominently a half century later by a new generation of justices who proceeded to move constitutional law and judicial policy making in the direction prematurely favored by Harlan.

On the Rehnquist Court, Justice Scalia's opinions have sometimes been influential in shaping the law. His advocacy on behalf of textualist interpretation of statutes has gained notice from both legal scholars and Congress. As described in Chapter 2, his opinions on free exercise of religion and the Eighth Amendment produced major changes in constitutional law when he managed to garner sufficient support from his colleagues to write majority opinions. More often, however, Scalia is not chosen by the chief justice or the senior justice in the majority to write on behalf of the Court, even when he is a member of the majority, and thus he asserts himself most frequently through concurring and dissenting opinions.

The ultimate influence of the substance of Scalia's reasoning and arguments remains to be seen. Justice William Brennan said that he wrote his dissents for future generations when he could not persuade his colleagues to adopt his views.[28] The same may hold true for Scalia, either by design or by happenstance. Whether or not Scalia intends to write for future generations, if future presidential elections produce conservative presidents, then yet-to-be-named conservative justices may look to the many forceful opinions written by Scalia as the source of ideas for justifying their decisions.

Individual justices also significantly influence the Supreme Court through their effectiveness in the Court's interactive decision-making processes. Chief Justice Earl Warren, for example, was well known for the leadership abilities that enabled him to draw the justices together on many issues.[29] Justice Brennan was considered to be an exceptionally effective politician within the Court who was sensitive to the viewpoints and feelings of his colleagues and who could use his sensitivity and interpersonal communication skills to develop opinions that would attract majority support.[30]

The foregoing mechanisms through which individual justices significantly influence the Supreme Court—namely casting decisive votes in divided cases, authoring persuasive opinions, and exercising leadership or strategic political skills in interacting with other justices—have all been the subjects of previous studies by scholars. By contrast, Justice Scalia has established himself as influential through a less noticed mechanism for significant impact: repelling potential allies through opinions and actions that clash with the Court's usual collegial, interactive decision-making processes. As one observer remarked about Scalia, "this is a magnet that repels rather than attracts."[31]

Obviously, Scalia intentionally refuses to engage in diplomatic behavior or strategic interactions in order to persuade his colleagues to join his opinions. His rigid, clear-sighted view of constitutional law prevents him from considering the possibility of participating in the inevitable compromises that underlie majority opinions produced when justices engage in give-and-take interactions in order to form stable majorities. In Geoffrey Stone's words, "[Scalia] believes he has the true faith, the real understanding of the Constitution, and that others who basically agree with him don't have the guts to follow through."[32] Although Scalia pursues his jurisprudential path deliberately, he probably never anticipated that his strident, individualistic style would actually help to defeat his persistent efforts to attain his objectives.

Scalia's impact on key decisions has shaped the legacy of the Rehnquist Court. On paper, political conservatives had an unsurpassed opportunity to reshape constitutional law and judicial policy making. Through timely success in presidential elections, Republicans controlled the White House during every year that a new justice was appointed to the Supreme Court for an era spanning nearly a quarter of a century (1969–1993). Moreover, presidents committed to conservatism made five appointments to the Supreme Court during the relatively brief span of one decade. From Justice O'Connor's appointment by President Reagan in 1981 to Justice Thomas's appointment by President Bush in 1991, a majority of the Supreme Court's members were appointed with the specific intention of adding conservative justices who would combat the liberal policy decisions produced during the Warren and Burger Court eras. Scholars were quick to note that all of the elements of the Supreme Court were coming together to favor conservative interests:

The appointment of an astute, forceful, and ideological chief justice [i.e., Rehnquist] who has regularly opposed the civil-liberties orientation of the Court, the emergence of an ostensibly cohesive conservative bloc on the Court, and some initial [case decisions] from the Court itself all point in [the] direction [of a new, consistent conservatism].[33]

Yet even when the Court's lone Democrat, Justice White, supported the conservative justices' attacks against precedents concerning abortion, school prayer, and criminal defendants' rights, a majority of justices on the Supreme Court declined to fulfill political conservatives' long-held dream of reversing controversial liberal precedents. During the Rehnquist Court era, the Supreme Court made many conservative decisions affecting prisoners' rights and other issues. With respect to such key issues as abortion and school prayer, however, as conservative justices reacted negatively to Justice Scalia's judicial behavior, the Court stopped short of reversing the liberal jurisprudential tides set in motion during the 1950s, 1960s, and 1970s.

The distinguishing feature of a "moment" as a matter of temporal terminology is that a moment ends. Moreover, it often ends too quickly to suit those who looked forward to it. The election of a Democratic president in November 1992 gave a liberal, Bill Clinton, the power to replace any of the aging justices who would choose to retire or who would succumb to age or illness. Clinton's election, the March 1993 announcement of the impending retirement of dependable conservative Justice Byron White, and news media reports emanating from the Court that two more elderly justices, Harry Blackmun and John Paul Stevens, may plan to retire during Clinton's first term caused the publicly recognized end of the conservatives' moment of opportunity.[34] The addition of younger, more liberal justices is certain to change the balance of ideological power and the decision-making dynamics within the high court. Clinton's election was not, however, the event that ended the conservatives' glorious opportunity. The moment ended in June 1992 when Justices Kennedy, O'Connor, and Souter reacted against their colleague Justice Scalia and announced to the world that, with respect to the key policy issues of abortion and separation of church and state, the efforts of Presidents Reagan and Bush to reshape the Supreme Court had gone for naught.

Future presidents who wish to shape the Supreme Court's composition in order to advance their policy preferences might draw several lessons from the example of the Rehnquist Court. If the suddenly more moderate judicial conservatives, such as Justice Kennedy, are viewed as inconsistent or as having changed their philosophical viewpoints, then future presidents might simply resign themselves to the lesson learned by Dwight Eisenhower in the appointments of Chief Justice Warren and Justice Brennan: Justices' future decision-making behavior is unpredictable. However, if a president looked more deeply into the Rehnquist Court to see how the human beings with black robes interacted with, and reacted to, each other, the president might recognize a new lesson from the example of Ronald Reagan's appointment of Justice Scalia: It is not sufficient to appoint a justice who is intelligent, creative, articulate, and forceful. Because the Supreme Court's decisions are produced by the persuasive interactions of the justices, effective justices must recognize and accept that decision making within a collegial court involves strategic interactions, cooperation, compromise, and the other elements of *political* behavior. Despite public denials by judicial officers, these very elements characterize human beings' actions in courts as well as in other authoritative institutions.

NOTES

1. Harmelin v. Michigan, 111 S. Ct. 2680 (1991).

2. Paul M. Barrett, "Despite Expectations, Scalia Fails to Unify Conservatives on Court," *Wall Street Journal*, 28 April 1992, p. A1.

3. Harmelin v. Michigan, 111 S. Ct. 2680, 2702 (1991) (Kennedy, J., concurring in part and concurring in the judgment).

4. See C. Neal Tate, "Personal Attribute Models of Voting Behavior of U.S. Supreme Court Justices: Liberalism in Civil Liberties and Economics Decisions, 1946–1978," *American Political Science Review* 75 (1981): 355–367; Jeffrey A. Segal, "Supreme Court Justices as Human Decision Makers: An Individual Level Analysis of Search and Seizure Cases," *Journal of Politics* 48 (1986): 938–955; Saul Brenner and John F. Krol, "Strategies in Certiorari Voting on the United States Supreme Court," *Journal of Politics* 51 (1989): 828–840.

5. Lee Epstein and Joseph Kobylka, *The Supreme Court and Legal Change* (Chapel Hill: University of North Carolina Press, 1992), p. 310.

6. Rust v. Sullivan, 111 S. Ct. 1759 (1991).

7. Planned Parenthood v. Casey, 112 S. Ct. 2791 (1992).

8. Lee v. Weisman, 112 S. Ct. 2649 (1992).

9. Linda Greenhouse, "Justices Define Limits of Own Power," *New York Times*, 22 November 1991, p. A8.

10. Ibid.

11. Christopher E. Smith, *Critical Judicial Nominations and Political Change: The Impact of Clarence Thomas* (Westport, Conn.: Praeger, 1993), chap. 3.

12. Christopher E. Smith and Scott Patrick Johnson, "The First-Term Performance of Justice Clarence Thomas," *Judicature* 76 (1993): 174.

13. Richard Lacayo, "Inside the Court," *Time*, 13 July 1992, p. 29.

14. Timothy M. Phelps and Helen Winternitz, *Capitol Games* (New York: Hyperion, 1992), p. xv.

15. Virginia Lamp Thomas, "Breaking Silence," *People*, 11 November 1991, pp. 108, 111.

16. Neil A. Lewis, "Law Professor Accuses Thomas of Sexual Harassment in 1980's," *New York Times*, 7 October 1991, p. A1.

17. Karen O'Connor, "The Effects of the Thomas Appointment to the Supreme Court," *P.S.: Political Science and Politics* 25 (1992): 492, 495.

18. David A. Kaplan, "An Uncomfortable Seat," *Newsweek*, 28 October 1991, p. 31.

19. Linda Greenhouse, "Trying to Define Clarence Thomas," *New York Times*, 15 September 1991, p. 17.

20. "Excerpts from Senate Hearings on the Thomas Nomination," *New York Times*, 12 September 1991, p. A10.

21. Smith and Johnson, "The First-Term Performance," p. 174.

22. Thomas Sancton, "Judging Thomas," *Time*, 13 July 1992, p. 30.

23. "The Justices Scold Thomas," *Time*, 9 March 1992, p. 31.

24. Hudson v. McMillian, 112 S. Ct. 995 (1992).

25. "Thomas: Hypocritic Oath?" *Newsweek*, 9 March 1992, p. 6.

26. Paul M. Barrett, "On the Right: Thomas Is Emerging As a Strong Conservative Out to Prove Himself," *Wall Street Journal*, 26 April 1993, p. A4.

27. Christopher E. Smith and Scott P. Johnson, "Newcomer on the High Court: Justice Souter and the Supreme Court's 1990 Term," *South Dakota Law Review* 37 (1992): 39–41.

28. Linda Greenhouse, "Supreme Court Dissenters: Loners or Pioneers?" *New York Times*, 20 July 1990, p. B7.

29. David Danelski, "The Influence of the Chief Justice in the Decisional Process of the Supreme Court," in *American Court Systems*, eds. Sheldon Goldman and Austin Sarat (New York: Longman, 1989), pp. 489–490.

30. Linda Greenhouse, "An Activist's Legacy," *New York Times*, 22 July 1990, pp. 1, 22.

31. Tony Mauro, "High Court Adjourns for Summer Intact," *Legal Times*, 9 July 1990, p. 10.

32. Greenhouse, "Supreme Court Dissenters," p. B7.

33. Charles Lamb and Stephen Halpern, "The Burger Court and Beyond," in *The Burger Court: Political and Judicial Profiles*, eds. Charles Lamb and Stephen Halpern (Champaign: University of Illinois Press, 1991), p. 455.

34. Linda Greenhouse, "White Announces He'll Step Down from High Court," *New York Times*, 20 March 1993, p. 1.

Select Bibliography

Abraham, Henry J. *Justices and Presidents: A Political History of Appointments to the Supreme Court*, 2nd ed. New York: Oxford University Press, 1985.

Baum, Lawrence. *The Supreme Court*, 4th ed. Washington, D.C.: Congressional Quarterly Press, 1992.

Blasecki, Janet. "Justice Lewis F. Powell: Swing Voter or Staunch Conservative?" *Journal of Politics* 52 (1990): 530–547.

Brisbin, Richard A., Jr. "The Conservatism of Antonin Scalia," *Political Science Quarterly* 105 (1990): 1–29.

Caplan, Lincoln. *The Tenth Justice: The Solicitor General and the Rule of Law*. New York: Random House, 1987.

Johnson, Scott P. and Christopher E. Smith. "David Souter's First Term on the Supreme Court: The Impact of a New Justice," *Judicature* 75 (1992): 238–243.

Kannar, George. "The Constitutional Catechism of Antonin Scalia," *Yale Law Journal* 99 (1990): 1297–1357.

Kingdon, John W. *Agendas, Alternatives, and Public Policies*. Boston: Little, Brown, 1984.

Meaux, Jean Morgan. "Justice Antonin Scalia and Judicial Restraint: A Conservative Resolution of Conflict between Individual and State," *Tulane Law Review* 62 (1987): 233–237.

Murphy, Walter F. *Elements of Judicial Strategy*. Chicago: University of Chicago Press, 1964.

O'Brien, David. *Storm Center: The Supreme Court in American Politics*, 2nd ed. New York: W. W. Norton, 1990.

Savage, David G. *Turning Right: The Making of the Rehnquist Court.* New York: John Wiley & Sons, 1992.

Scalia, Antonin. "Originalism: The Lesser Evil," *University of Cincinnati Law Review* 57 (1989): 856–864.

———. "The Disease as Cure," *Washington University Law Quarterly* (1979): 147–154.

Schwartz, Herman. *Packing the Courts: The Conservative Campaign to Rewrite the Constitution.* New York: Charles Scribners' Sons, 1988.

Smith, Christopher E. *Critical Judicial Nominations and Political Change: The Impact of Clarence Thomas.* Westport, Conn.: Praeger, 1993.

———. "Justice Antonin Scalia and Criminal Justice Cases," *Kentucky Law Journal* 81 (1992–93): 187–212.

———. "The Supreme Court in Transition: Assessing the Legitimacy of the Leading Legal Institution," *Kentucky Law Journal* 79 (1990–91): 317–346.

———. "Justice Antonin Scalia and the Institutions of American Government," *Wake Forest Law Review* 25 (1990): 783–809.

Smith, Christopher E. and Linda Fry. "Vigilance or Accommodation: The Changing Supreme Court and Religious Freedom," *Syracuse Law Review* 42 (1991): 893–944.

Smith, Christopher E. and Scott Patrick Johnson. "The First-Term Performance of Justice Clarence Thomas," *Judicature* 76 (1993): 172–178.

———. "Newcomer on the High Court: Justice Souter and the Supreme Court's 1990 Term," *South Dakota Law Review* 37 (1992): 21–43.

Wilson, James G. "Constraints of Power: The Constitutional Opinions of Judges Scalia, Bork, Posner, Easterbrook and Winter," *University of Miami Law Review* 40 (1986): 1171–1266.

Index

About the Author

CHRISTOPHER E. SMITH is an Associate Professor of Political Science at the University of Akron. He is the author of six books, including most recently, *Critical Judicial Nominations and Political Change: The Impact of Clarence Thomas* (Praeger, 1993).